CHRISTMAS CAROLS

∴ CHRISTMAS CAROLS ∴

A History of our Favourite
Christmas Carols, from
Village Green to Church Choir

Andrew Gant

P
PROFILE BOOKS

This paperback edition published in 2016

First published in Great Britain in 2014 by
PROFILE BOOKS LTD
3 Holford Yard
Bevin Way
London WC1X 9HD
www.profilebooks.com

1 3 5 7 9 10 8 6 4 2

Printed and bound in Great Britain by
CPI Group (UK) Ltd, Croydon CR0 4YY

A CIP catalogue record for this book is available from the British Library.

ISBN 978 1 78125 353 3
eISBN 978 1 78283 109 9

·: Contents :·

·: Introduction :·

nglish Christmas carols are a hotchpotch, like the English themselves. Perhaps that's why they are so popular. They have the power to summon up a special kind of midwinter mood, like the aroma of mince pies and mulled wine and the twinkle of lights on a tree. It's a kind of magic.

How did they get that magic? Most of these songs were not composed as Christmas carols. Many were not 'composed' at all. Almost all did not begin life with the words they have now. Some didn't have words at all. Several evolved from folk songs: some are evolving still. One much-loved carol started out as a song about a delinquent farm-boy and a couple of dead cows. Many of the most 'English' carols have at least one ancestor in another country, in the mountains of Austria, or nineteenth-century America, or a Pyrenean hillside, in Lutheran psalters, handsome volumes of illuminated plainsong or sturdy hymnbooks from Finland, first opened by the flickering light of a fire in some stone hall one dark evening, deep in the sixteenth century.

The origins of the word 'carol' are almost as murky as the history of some of the tunes themselves. Most European languages, living and dead, have been quoted as the source of the word, though most writers agree that there is a dash of French in there somewhere.

In the beginning, a 'carol' was a celebratory song, with dancing. There is no exclusive connection to Christmas. Music is in the traditional 'stanza and burden' (or 'verse and refrain') format. It certainly has nothing to do with church. In about 1400, the gory tale of 'Sir Gawain and the Green Knight', as translated by J. R. R.Tolkien, tells us

> The king lay at Camelot at Christmas-tide with many a lovely lord … to the court they came at carols to play … they danced and danced on, and dearly they carolled.

Choirs sang church music. Everyone else sang carols. Tolkien's version of 'Sir Gawain' draws the distinction between 'songs of delight, such as canticles of Christmas' and 'carol-dances'.

Folk carols on Christian themes were sung in the field and the graveyard, and on semi-magical processions round the parish. Their texts often cover the entire Christian world-view, from creation to resurrection. Today, we tend to just snip out the bits we want at Christmas, for example 'Tomorrow shall be my dancing day' and 'The cherry-tree carol', which was not how our mediaeval forebears used these songs at all.

Fifteenth-century English carols began to take on some of the sophistication of the church composer. The texts are 'macaronic', freely dropping Latin words and phrases into an English lyric:

> There is no rose of such vertu
> As is the rose that bare Jesu.
> *Res Miranda.*

The music is in the ubiquitous verse-and-refrain format.

By the sixteenth century, the word 'carol' could find itself loosely applied to any song with a seasonal connection, still definitely not just Christmas. An ancient and mysterious folk song appeared under the title 'Corpus Christi Carol' in 1504. Court composer William Cornysh was paid the handsome sum of £20.00 for 'setting of a Carrall upon Xmas day' at around the same time as Wynkyn de Worde included the entirely secular 'Carol of hunting' in the collection which he (rather confusingly) called 'Christmasse carolles' in 1521. One of William Byrd's consort songs from around the 1580s, designed to be sung at home, has the sub-title 'A Caroll for New-Yeares Day'. A text sung in church at Christmas could also be a 'carol', whether the words make any reference to the Nativity or not: a 1630 publication refers to 'Certain of David's Psalmes intended for Christmas Carolls fitted to the most common but solempne Tunes'. These 'Carolls' are just the psalms of the day. Neither words nor music have any seasonal content.

Protestants wanted to grab the best tunes back from the devil and the pub. During the Reformation, secular songs and well-known chorales started to be used in worship. Compilers of tunes for psalm singing, hugely influential and popular, put them in their psalters. Alongside this went a passion for education. School songbooks sprang up everywhere. One such book, *Piae Cantiones ecclesiasticae velerum episcoporum*, is the source of a large number of our best-known carols. In France, dancing-masters and *chefs du choeur* started noting down little rustic *Noëls* and incorporating them into published collections, for teaching, playing, dancing and singing, and sometimes adding new words. All feed into the tradition we have today.

In the mid seventeenth century a more extreme brand of Protestantism took hold in England, with its stern disapproval of any kind of levity in church, or indeed anywhere else. The Puritans, famously, banned Christmas. As always, though, we need to see this in context. Puritans banned a lot of things. Christmas was not the mad, musical midwinter party we have come to know since. It went as part of a general assault on saints' days and elaborate ritual in church practice as a whole, and as part of a rather arcane dispute about which took precedence when a liturgical fast fell on the same day as Christmas. The jollity, of course, came back in a great whirl of enthusiasm at the Restoration in 1660. Carols, like life, were mainly an excuse for having fun. Songs about drinking, wassailing, drinking, eating, dancing and drinking were especially popular.

The more measured Protestantism of the very last Stuarts, William, Mary and Anne, made its own distinctive contribution. The beginnings of congregational hymn singing in the eighteenth century give us familiar carols like 'While Shepherds Watched', still closely based on the old style of metrical psalm singing. These words have been sung to all sorts of different tunes, each one reflecting the social and religious preoccupations of the singers. The Wesleys and Watts gave their followers lengthy devotions to sing on the dusty road, which have been absorbed into the popular consciousness. Watts's lovely 'Cradle Song' turns up, suitably distorted by the Chinese whispers of an oral tradition, as the words of an English folk song. Parish churches, with their distinctive bands of instrumentalists and 'West Gallery' choirs, mixed fashionable metropolitan musical style with a love of hymn singing and their own intensely local traditions to create something sturdy, uniquely English and full of character.

In the mid nineteenth century, antiquarians and folklorists like William Chappell began to collect and publish their native folk songs. There are several important books devoted just to Christmas carols. Joshua Sylvester (a pseudonym) illustrates this new spirit of historical enquiry, and acknowledges some of its pioneers, in the introduction to his own 1864 book:

> Forty years ago an antiquary wrote complainingly; 'Carols begin to be spoken of as not belonging to this century, and yet no one, as I am aware of, has attempted a collection of these fugitives'. Several gleaners since then, however, have entered the field, Mr. Davies Gilbert, Mr. Sandys, Dr. Rimbault, and Mr. Thomas Wright have each garnered their gleanings into little volumes. From these I have derived much assistance in the compilation of the present work.

Sandys has turned out to be the most fruitful for our modern carol tradition, though, as Sylvester acknowledges, these early books overlap a good deal.

These men were compilers, working from existing sources like ballad sheets or the libraries of earlier collectors. The next stage, in the early twentieth century, was for the new generation of 'gleaners' to go out into the highways and byways and hear folk carols for themselves. Cecil Sharp explains how it's done:

> Only a few weeks ago I asked two old men who were singing to me whether they knew a certain carol. One of them said that he did; the other, the elder of the two,

shook his head doubtfully. Whereupon the younger singer stood up and, dragging his companion up beside him, said encouragingly: 'Stand up, and think you've got snow in your boots, and it'll come to you all right.' And it did!

Most of the early books and ballad sheets didn't contain tunes. The oral tradition was so well established, you could happily assume your reader would already know them. Often it was enough simply to print the name of the tune, or, if the words were in a common metre, allow the singer to use any matching tune which he already knew. This contributed to the huge variety and lack of standardisation about which tune goes with a particular text. Even when the same tune was used in different towns and villages, it could differ between one and the other. The same tune could exist in scores of versions, alike in essentials, quite different in detail. When Sharp and others started writing down the tunes as people actually sang them, it became clear how an oral tradition militates against uniformity. Stainer's 'God rest you merry, gentlemen' has a different first note from Sharp's (the first degree of the scale instead of the fifth). Stainer got the tune from the streets of London. Sharp collected it in Cambridge. That interval of fifty miles shows up as the musical interval of a perfect fifth.

Some 'folk songs' may well also involve the presence of a real author or composer. Sharp wrote:

> In several parts of England I have found carols which are peculiar to certain villages, by the inhabitants of which they are regarded as private possessions of great value, to be jealously guarded and retained for their own use. These are not traditional or folk carols but the elementary

' ... *discordant caterwauling* ...': *carol-singing in
London. The ubiquitous ballad broadside sheets
have words and pictures, but no tunes.*

compositions of simple musicians, very possibly of those who in the old days were members of the Church bands. They are easily distinguished from the popular carol by the formal nature of the music and words, and also by the fact that many of them are written in parts. Some of these compositions are by no means without merit. The melodies, if not inspired, are usually strong and sincere, and, plainly, the expression of genuine feeling.

He quotes one, which, 'while it lacks the freshness, the *naiveté*, and indeed pretty nearly all the typical and character-istic qualities of the folk carol, is nevertheless quite as good as some, and far better than many of the modern Christmas hymns annually sung in fashionable Churches and Chapels', adding, 'there is, perhaps, no branch of folk-music in the creation of which the unconscious art of the peasant is seen to greater advantage than the carol'.

His tone appears slightly condescending to modern ears, but Sharp, king of the collectors, was unquestionably 'strong and sincere', and a scholar.

The dedicated idealism of Sharp, Lucy Broadwood, J. A. Fuller-Maitland and others is of crucial importance in the story of the carol (although even then the word 'carol' had not taken on its exclusively Christmassy connotation: a 1903 book specifically refers to 'Easter carols and Christmas songs', and an important publication of 1924 collects what it calls *Fifty-two Songs for Christmas, Easter, and Other Seasons* under the catch-all title *The Cambridge Carol-Book*.)

Many carols are clearly local variations or expansions on authored originals. Some have an artfulness which, as Sharp suggests, implies the existence of an author but with no clue as to who might have done the deed. Translations complicate

Carol singing in the country: much more genteel.

things further, not just between languages, but from one style of religious practice or one century to another. Many fall between the cracks or slip down the back of the pew. So, if you occasionally get to the end of a chapter in this book slightly unsure about who wrote words or tune or bits of either: me too. It's all part of the tradition.

Collecting songs in the field also, of course, exposes you to the vagaries of the various performers you happen to meet. Writing in the 1920s, Marjorie Kennedy-Fraser refers to the work of the Rev. Patrick Macdonald of Kilmore, Argyll, who published a book of two hundred airs in 1784:

> Apropos of the luck of the collector in hearing the best versions of airs, Macdonald remarks that in noting the tunes, 'perhaps he has not always given the best sets of them, as he may not have had the good fortune to hear those sets...When he had frequent opportunities of hearing an air, he chose that set which appeared to him the best, the most genuine. When he had not such opportunities, he satisfied himself with writing the notes which he heard.

There is an element of choice, of editing, in what the collector does. Vaughan Williams takes this one stage further, regarding his published versions of tunes as a further variant, and allowing himself to add or smooth out musical details: the long note before the last line of 'O Little Town of Bethlehem', for example, is his invention. Mr Garman of Forest Green didn't sing it like that.

This creative unreliability of the field collection comes vividly into focus when technology allowed collectors to start making sound-recordings around the beginning of the twentieth century. Thanks to the wonderful British Library sound archive, we can listen to the crackling sounds of men and women, some of whom watched as children when the lads of their village marched off to fight Boney, singing carols and slurping tea. Often, memories are remarkable. Sometimes melodies get muddled and songs stutter to a stop. Husbands and wives have a little bicker about what comes next. Regional accents can be completely impenetrable.

The fruits of these 'gleanings' are priceless in every sense. As late as the 1970s, the great folklorist Roy Palmer is collecting variants of carols, and the stories to go with them, including the man who enjoyed going to the pub on Sunday afternoons in the 1940s, where he learnt a local variant of 'While Shepherds Watched' from a man called Bill, who was 'a carpenter, but he didn't like work, Bill. He preferred to get his living by sleight of hand, and he avoided work like the plague'. The story ends 'we used to go up there, and I started to learn to play the banjo. And then I met my wife, and I gave it up'. Of such is history.

So far, much of this has nothing to do with church. The liturgy, the content of divine worship, was prescribed by law and was no place for most of these irreverent impostors.

In the nineteenth century the church began to make a distinctive contribution of its own. The clergy played a crucial role as editors, translators, composers, arrangers and authors. A number of familiar items were newly written in America. The stirring congregational tub-thumper, and the organ to go with it, were the invention of the Victorians.

Their successors, perhaps prudently, sought to ameliorate some of its excesses. The Introduction to the English

Hymnal of 1906 comments rather sniffily: 'a large body of voices singing together makes a distinctly artistic effect, though that of each individual voice might be the opposite. And it may be added that a desire to parade a trained choir often accompanies a debased musical taste.' Clear echoes here of Sharp's reservations about the artistic value of the Christmas music in 'fashionable churches'.

Carol singing used to belong in the street far more than in the pew. The sight of carol singers merrily tramping from door to door has vanished to such an extent that we can easily forget just how familiar and widespread the practice was, until surprisingly recently. The carol used to be an outdoors creature, a farmyard animal as much as a domestic pet. Here's one account from 1869:

> Having spent some part of my Christmas holidays in a retired little town in Gloucestershire, where many old customs and superstitions still linger, I of course came in for a good share of carol-singing. These, however, differed very much from the irreverent and discordant caterwauling (I cannot call it anything else) which greet our ears evening after evening in our suburban streets. For irreverent they could not well be, since sacred words were not attempted, and discordant they certainly were not, seeing that the singers were composed chiefly of the members of the choir.

For all his *hauteur*, the writer captures well the types and sheer irrepressible ubiquity of *al fresco* singing in both town and country, and the carefree mixture of sacred and secular which forms the repertoire of these rude mechanicals.

Even as late as 1958, the hymnologist and carol historian

Erik Routley can say that 'there is no doubt that carol-singing is more popular and more widespread an activity in this country at the present time than it ever was before'. Wouldn't it be fun if we could learn to do this again?

And, still, the idea remains that a Christmas carol is in some respects a thing not quite proper for church. As late as 1971, Roy Palmer interviewed an elderly couple who sang him their local tune to 'While Shepherds Watched'.

'Where did you learn that?' Palmer asks.

'Round the streets. That was sung by carol-singers, when we went round collecting the pennies,' is the reply. 'But we never heard that sung in church. They're very traditional, in church.'

'So, the church wouldn't have that?' asks Palmer.

'No, they just sing the ordinary "While Shepherds Watched", the thing out of the hymn book.'

You can hear the shock in her voice. The very idea.

At the same time, carols began to be considered worthy of academic attention. Early twentieth-century scholars put their texts in anthologies. The American linguist and philologist, Edith Rickert, included several hundred lyrics, meticulously sourced and edited, in her monumental 1910 publication *English Folk Carols 1400–1700* (though, in fact, her earliest examples are some two hundred years earlier than this). Rickert's introduction, helpfully classifying traditional carols into types, as Sylvester had done, is still a model of scholarship. Erik Routley wrote as well as anyone about the subject. His book is not as well known as it deserves. He is funny, humane, thoughtful, and the only writer man enough to acknowledge in print that 'The First Nowell' is 'really a rather terrible tune'. Hear, hear.

Thanks to publications like the *English Hymnal*, the two 'University' carol books and the *Cowley Carol Book*, the twentieth century came to value the inclusivity of a body of songs which everybody knew. The old distinction between indoor and outdoor carols was largely gone. Items which are more properly Christmas hymns are printed and sung alongside traditional Christmas carols. The editors of these books, like Luther, knew how to value a good tune, from wherever it comes, while still attempting to scrub off the remaining patina of 'debased' Victorian sentimentality. The attempt continues.

Christmas carols are, perhaps, the nearest thing we still have to a folk tradition – an oral tradition. We know them because we know them. We never really learnt them, they've just always been there. This gives the tradition a particularly fluid quality, able to absorb influences from all over the place, but never quite settling into a finished format.

How does the second verse of 'O Little Town of Bethlehem' actually go? Or the last verse of 'Away In a Manger'? Is it 'stay by my side until morning is nigh', or 'stay by my bedside till morning is nigh'? The poet must have written one or the other, surely?

Is there a passing-note at 'now in flesh ap-pea-ear-ring' or not? If not, why does everybody sing it? Should we try and stop them? How?

And, is it 'Of the Father's *Heart* Begotten', or '*Love* Begotten'? At least when we're working with the published words of a well-known author we must be singing the words in an accepted, 'correct' version, mustn't we? Well, no. Charles Wesley didn't write 'Hark, the Herald Angels Sing', he wrote 'Hark, How all the Welkin Rings'. So why don't we sing it like that? Why do we sing carols in the versions we do? Because we just do. These tunes, gathered together like outcasts from all over the world, have taken on what Philip Larkin calls 'the whiff of bands and organ-pipes and myrrh' and taken their place around our festive table where children listen, ready to carry them on to the next generation and beyond.

When we sing our favourite carols at Christmas, we may think we're taking part in a long, unbroken, and unchanging tradition. This book shows the extent to which that is true: which is not very. There are lots of good stories and engaging characters, from the greatest musicians and thinkers to shepherd boys, choirboys, monks and drunks. The best characters are the songs themselves, absorbed from their origins into the most profound and atavistic vein of Englishness. There is music, and a specially made CD recording to accompany this book. There are tunes you will know, and some you won't. There are some you might be surprised to find in a carol book ('On Ilkley Moor bah 'tat'? Where's that?'). And there are lots more where these came from.

Enjoy exploring this unique and special part of our heritage.

Happy Christmas!

1

·: The Angel Gabriel :·

We start on a hillside, not in Judea but in Spain, watching an angel with 'wings as drifted snow'.

That gorgeous image tells us a lot about our Christmas carol tradition. It's not in the Bible. It's not even in the original carol. It was written by a Victorian clergyman, standing (not sitting) at his desk in his vicarage in Devon.

That's how these things come down to us, as surprising and as beautiful as the angel itself.

'The Angel Gabriel' is a folk carol from the Basque country. It was collected by the composer Charles Bordes and published in the series *Archives de la tradition basque* in 1895. Bordes represents an important type of musician in this story; inquiring, creative, historically and culturally aware. He instituted the performance of Italian Renaissance music at his grand society church in Paris, pioneered the rediscovery and performance of plainsong, and founded the Schola Cantorum to promote his ideas. At the same time, he was fascinated by the folk culture of the regions of his native France, collecting traditional texts and melodies before the rapid changes of the new century swept them away. It is a story repeated all over Europe. His equivalents in England were the ragged band of skilled musicians and folklorists led by Ralph Vaughan Williams and Cecil Sharp, and a group of clergymen who wanted to raid and preserve the inheritance of their Catholic forebears as much as the earthier devotions of their parish, in order to bring the best and most beautiful music from across Europe and beyond into their newly confident church. These men were the warrior-priests on the cultural and liturgical front line. Many were of strong and decided character. None more so than Sabine Baring-Gould.

Baring-Gould spent much of his childhood travelling in Europe, partly because of a recurring bronchial complaint which did not prevent him growing up to father fifteen children and live to the age of nearly ninety. As a young curate in York, he fell in love with a fourteen-year-old mill girl called Grace Taylor, who was sent to learn middle-class manners in the home of a local family until she was old enough to marry (a similar marital arrangement was used by E. W. Benson, later Archbishop of Canterbury and inventor of the carol service, with colourful results). Grace and Sabine were married for forty-eight years, and when she died he inscribed the words *Dimidium Animae Meae* ('Half my Soul') on her tomb. All but one of their children survived to adulthood.

In 1872, Baring-Gould's father died, and he inherited the 3,000-acre family estate of Lew Trenchard in Devon. The living of the local parish church was, naturally, in the gift of the squire, and when it fell vacant in 1881 he appointed himself. The transition to landed squire-parson was complete, and he dedicated the rest of his long life to the people and buildings of his parish and to the voracious pursuit of his own all-encompassing interests.

Educated Victorians believed they could do anything. Professional specialisation is a later invention. This was an era when a headmaster could pupate into a bishop and vice versa; when a gardener like Joseph Paxton could set out to construct a glass-house for a newly discovered giant lily and end up as a pioneering artist-engineer in glass and iron; when Brunel could design anything he liked; when men like Darwin and Huxley were draughtsmen and prose stylists as well as scientists and adventurers.

Baring-Gould was interested in everything. When his church and manor house needed rebuilding, he acted as his own architect. He travelled, he studied, he investigated. Above all, he wrote: novels, libretti, books about saints, stone circles, werewolves and ghosts. He wrote hymns, including that stirring torch-song of muscular Christianity, 'Onward, Christian Soldiers' (later set to a tune by, of course, Arthur Sullivan. Who else?). Baring-Gould's literary output is estimated at over 1,250 titles, an astonishing number which, even assuming a rather unlikely active writing career of sixty years, works out at one every two to three weeks. Naturally, he did things his own way: he had a desk specially made, which enabled him to write standing up, which he did to the very end of his life.

He was, by any standards, a fine writer. Modern scholarship may, perhaps, question if such rapidity allowed for the most detailed primary research. Serious theology may wonder at his cheerfully egalitarian approach to the lives and influence of saints of the church, the hounds of Dartmoor and the coveys of ancient Kings under their tors and tumuli. But his use of language, his range of reference and his sheer enthusiasm more than make up for any such deficiencies. Like those great Reformation stylists of the English language from whom he clearly learnt so much, he was a communicator.

On one of his youthful peregrinations, Baring-Gould spent a winter in and around the Basque region, and later wrote about the area in *A Book of the Pyrenees*. All his voluminous inclusivity is here, snapping up every trifle of history and prehistory: the Romans, Bonaparte, wild flowers, geology, language, architecture and costume, constantly cross-referencing them with his observations and readings about other parts of Europe. Fascinatingly, he regarded the Basques as part of a family of Celtic peoples of which he, a native of Devon, was also a part, 'the last shrunken remains of that Iberian race that once occupied all Western Europe from Scotland to Portugal and Spain'. He is not always particularly polite about the Basque. He compares the language to Gaelic, Welsh, French, Latin and even Chinese, and concludes that 'his own language, as represented by the Basque of the present day, is crude, unformed and wanting in flexibility'. He states that 'the Basque has not distinguished himself in literature', dismissing a set of ancient poems as forgeries. He even, in a strikingly modern passage, ticks them off roundly for the deforestation of their mountain slopes, pointing out that such environmental degradation is quick to achieve but slow to repair (and quoting the Sermon on the Mount in support of his argument, which the modern environmentalist would probably do well to avoid).

By his own estimation, one of his most important achievements was the collection of folk songs of Devon and Cornwall which he made in collaboration with a number of musical colleagues, including Cecil Sharp, and published in a series of books including *Songs and Ballads of the West*, *A Garland of Country Song*, and *English Folk-songs for Schools*. This last volume remained in regular use for much of the twentieth century. As a good clergyman, Baring-Gould found it necessary to tone down some of the ruder words (for example, the song 'Maids at Eighteen', where he blushingly dilutes the young lady's enthusiasm for certain aspects of the married estate, commenting 'however droll the words may be in the original, no girl would want to sing them today'). As a good scholar, however, he carefully preserved his original field notes, allowing later, less prudish generations to restore the song to its earthy glory.

His enthusiasms for Celtic culture and folk song come together in this beautiful carol. His text is as much a paraphrase as a direct translation, freely borrowing appropriate imagery from familiar English versions of the Magnificat and Ave Maria, as well as the mediaeval hymn 'Angelus ad Virginem', on which the folk song is based. Baring-Gould condenses the six verses of the Basque original into four, creating a touching dialogue between angel and virgin and moving from the Annunciation to its fulfilment at the Nativity in the last verse, all framed by a devoted little refrain with a clear echo of fifteenth-century English macaronic carols to the Virgin: 'most highly-favoured lady; *Gloria!*'.

He also indulges the curious habit shared with many of his clerical colleagues of inverting syntax in rather odd ways, something he would certainly not have allowed himself to do elsewhere in his admirably clear written output: 'for known a blessed mother thou shalt be'.

It's an odd quirk. They all did it, particularly the king of the carol writers, J. M. Neale. Some later writers and musicians hated it and soundly criticised them for it. But it has become very much part of how we do carols. Putting the words in an unusual order gives the text a kind of instant 'old-world' feel which seems appropriate, somehow. Attempts to change them back have usually failed. Perhaps our hymn writers, classical scholars all, were attempting at some level to impose the structures and virtues of Latin onto the vernacular, as grammarians have repeatedly tried to do to written English.

Like so many folk carols, the tune features a haunting, minor-flavoured mode and a liltingly irregular rhythm which refuses to go into a time signature: the first two phrases each have seven beats, the last two have eight, all in a gentle triple time which betrays its origins in something probably rather more rustic and dance-like.

The themes of our Christmas story are laid before us here. Its genesis reveals to us many of the themes of the story of our carol tradition. Like the angel, this little carol promises much.

'The Angel Gabriel'

The an-gel Ga-bri-el from hea-ven came,___ his wings as drift-ed snow, his eyes___ as flame. "All hail", said he, "thou low-ly maid-en Ma-ry,___ most high-ly fa-voured la-dy: *Glo - - - ri - a".*

'For known a blessed mother thou shalt be,
All generations laud and honour thee,
Thy Son shall be Emmanuel, by seers foretold
Most highly favoured lady,' Gloria!

Then gentle Mary meekly bowed her head
'To me be as it pleaseth God,' she said,
'My soul shall laud and magnify his holy name.'
Most highly favoured lady. Gloria!

Of her, Emmanuel, the Christ was born
In Bethlehem, all on a Christmas morn
And Christian folk throughout the world will ever say:
'Most highly favoured lady,' Gloria!

2

·: O Come, O Come Emmanuel :·

ome of our carols have become associated with celebrations of the birth of Jesus almost by accident. This one is bound into the liturgy and theology of Western Christianity since its earliest incarnations.

Its genesis lies in the 'seven 'O's', the great Advent antiphons. These are a series of prayers each invoking Christ by one of the names or titles he is given in scripture, ending with a supplication framed around that image. They are unimaginably ancient.

Boethius, the Roman author of *The Consolation of Philosophy* (whose writings about music gave mediaeval university students much grief), may show some familiarity with their language as far back as the early sixth century. The Anglo-Saxon poet Cynewulf wrote *The Christ* in about 750–800. Its first part, 'Advent', movingly intersperses the gospel narrative of Mary and Joseph with a series of reflections that clearly echo the language and imagery of the great 'O's (the edition and translation here are Sir Israel Gollancz's, published in London in 1892):

Eala þu reccend and þu riht cyning
Se þe locan healdeð lif ontyneð
Eadga us siges oþrum forwyrned
Wlitigan wil-siþes, gif his weorc ne deag.

O thou Ruler, and thou righteous King!
Thou Keeper of the keys that open life!
bless us with victory, with a bright career,
denied unto another, if his work is worthless!

The poem continues:

Eala earendel engla beorhtast
Ofer middan-geard monnum sended
And soðfæsta sunnan leoma,
Torht ofer tunglas. Þū tida gehwane
Of sylfum þe symle inlihtes.

Hail, heavenly beam, brightest of angels thou,
sent unto men upon this middle-earth!
Thou are the true refulgence of the sun,
radiant above the stars, and from thyself
illuminest for ever all the tides of time.

O thou God of spirits! how wisely thou
wast named, with name aright, Emmanuel!
as the angel spake the word in Hebrew first,
which in its secret meaning fully now
is thus interpreted: 'The Guardian of the skies,
God's Self, is now with us'.

(In passing, it was this edition that provided J. R. R. Tolkien with much of his imagery and several of his names, including Earendel and Middle Earth).

Later in the first millennium those great crucibles of liturgical music, the powerhouse Benedictine monasteries of Northern France, employed the Abbot as cantor for the first of the 'O's, with each subsequent antiphon being intoned on successive days by the next most senior member of the establishment in descending order of importance (an interesting inverted pre-echo of the modern habit of having the 'Nine Lessons' read in the opposite order of noteworthiness, the first by a nervous eight-year-old chorister trying to pretend he knows what a cicatrice is, then a student, right up to the local worthy).

Theologically, each antiphon links a prophecy of Isaiah through to its fulfilment in the gospel, echoing with the resonances of particular words and ideas through the Bible and beyond. Liturgically, the seven antiphons are sung before and after the Magnificat at Vespers on the last seven days of Advent (17–23 December). Remarkably, they survived and prospered into the Anglican and other Protestant traditions, though with some variation of the exact dates on which each is sung.

As with the gospels themselves, early Christian writers discovered (or created) several more to go with the original set. The basic set of seven each begin with the letter 'O', followed by the name or title being invoked: Sapientia; Adonai; Radix Jesse; Clavis David; Oriens; Rex Gentium; Emmanuel. Somebody noticed that the initial letters of these 'keywords', if read in reverse order, spell the Latin phrase 'Ero Cras', and claimed that this meant 'Tomorrow, I will come', in reference to the meaning of the season of Advent. Ingenious, but unlikely. For one thing, the phrase more accurately means 'Tomorrow I will be', which is at best rather vague. For another, this sort of word-play is not readily found in liturgical materials. Also, if it's a kind of hidden, coded prophecy building up to something, it spoils the point somewhat to do it backwards. More likely, some clever monk in the Middle Ages, an era which thoroughly enjoyed its acrostics, word-games and number patterns, noticed the coincidence one bored day at Vespers and set that particular hare running.

The theological exegesis of the antiphons has occupied the minds of many brainy people. Perhaps we may allow ourselves one tentative toe in these learned waters to get some small idea of where the words and ideas of this carol come from.

The first antiphon begins 'O Sapientia, quae ex ore Altissimi prodiisti ... veni ad docendum nos viam pruden-tiae' ('O Wisdom, proceeding from the mouth of the Highest ... come and teach us the way of understanding'). Isaiah says 'the spirit of Lord shall rest upon him, the spirit of wisdom and understanding'. The Wisdom of Solomon has 'wisdom reacheth from one end to another mightily: and sweetly doth she order all things'. Joshua was 'full of the spirit of wisdom'. The child Jesus 'grew, and waxed strong in spirit, filled with wisdom: and the grace of God was upon him'. St Paul asks 'that the Father of glory, may give unto you the spirit of wisdom and revelation in the knowledge of him'.

The words are pregnant with the promise of fulfilment, like Advent itself. This is the promise the antiphons, and their successor, the carol, seek to invoke.

The Advent antiphons are prose, with their own plainsong melody, and are still often sung by accomplished choirs. At some point they were versified into a regular metre and picked up a repeating refrain. The final stage was to marry them to an existing plainsong tune, originally intended for quite different words. A familiar classic emerges from the amalgamation of ancient, disparate elements.

Here is the Latin prose of the fourth antiphon:

O Clavis David, et sceptrum domus Israel: qui aperis, et nemo claudit; claudis, et nemo aperit: veni et educ vinctum de domo carceris, sedentem in tenebris, et umbra mortis.

(O key of David, and sceptre of the House of Israel, who opens, and no man shuts; who shuts, and no man opens: come and lead from the prison-house the captive who sits in darkness and in the shadow of death.)

And this is the metrical version, with its new refrain:

Veni, clavis Davidica!
Regna reclude caelica,
Fac iter tutum superum
Et claude vias inferum.
Gaude! Gaude! Emmanuel
Nascetur pro te, Israel.

The process by which the various versions merge and emerge is, of course, thoroughly hidden in the 'tenebris' and the 'umbra'. Finding a way through, introduces us to the work of unquestionably the two most important among the many Victorian clergymen in this story, John Mason Neale and Thomas Helmore.

Neale published the metrical Latin version, beginning 'Veni, veni, Emmanuel', in 1851. He believed that it was written in the twelfth century, with the refrain being added at an unknown later date. This is entirely credible on stylistic grounds, though the earliest source known to Neale, and indeed since, is a Tridentine Catholic Psalter from Cologne, dating from 1710. He set another historical puzzle with his choice of tune, harmonised by Helmore. Neale told his readers it was 'adapted from a French Missal'. The secret of exactly what that meant was to wait another hundred years for its own advent out of darkness.

Translators and hymnologists soon started scurrying all over this hymn, with its stirring evocation of the themes of Advent and its unusual but memorable melody. One of the very first English versions of the original antiphons was written, fittingly, by none other than the Captain of the Catholics himself, John Henry Newman, in 1836. Editors and compilers followed with multiple translations of the hymn, using the same metre as the Latin so their words could be sung to the same tune.

These versions went forth and multiplied so enthusiastically that the strands of their individual verbal DNA have got completely muddled up and become totally indistinguishable, like fruit-flies in a bell-jar. Writers borrow words and phrases from each other, with and without acknowledgement. Some hymn books ascribe their version to Neale, ignoring (or not noticing) the fact that they have altered his very first line from 'Draw nigh, draw nigh, Emmanuel' to 'O come, O come, Emmanuel'. Most give multiple attributions, to Neale, and Lacey, or the twelfth century, or Cologne, or anon, or unknown, or some combination of all these, usually adding the dreaded words 'and Editors' or 'and Compilers'. Some think 'Adonai' rhymes with 'majesty', others with 'earth and sky'. How *do* you pronounce that word? Who knows? Modern choirs don't. And what is a 'Dayspring'? And is it 'Emmanuel' or 'Immanuel'? – which are at least pronounced the same.

It's probably impossible to know now exactly who first wrote what. Verses mysteriously change their order like the French in a bus queue. Some assaults on the Latin, or bits of it, were committed by person or persons unknown. Enough, perhaps, for our purposes, to note that important contributions were made by, among many others, Neale, T. A. Lacey and Henry Sloane Coffin. The version given at the end of this chapter is Neale's, as adapted by Coffin and used in *Hymns Ancient and Modern*.

One other version merits attention. In the 1850s, Neale and Helmore published their *Hymnal Noted*. This is No. 65:

The interesting point here is the proper plainsong notation (four-line stave, old-style clef, rhythmless 'neumes' instead of crotchets and quavers, no bar lines), with English words. This is exactly what John Marbecke attempted at the Reformation. Respect the integrity of the old musical ways as much as possible, but give the people the words in their own language. The title of their hymn book may well contain an echo of Marbecke's famous publication *The Booke of Common Praier Noted* of 1550. As scholars, Neale and Helmore were ahead of their time.

Other editors, of course, forced the tune into the strait-jacket of a regular rhythmic pulse. It doesn't work. The tune won't go into 4/4, and arrangers have to keep chopping and changing their choice of time signature. All very confusing.

And what of the tune itself? Where did Neale get it from? *The Hymnal Noted* places the elusive French Missal, perhaps unexpectedly, in Lisbon. Neale spent the winter of 1853–4 in Madeira, recuperating from a lung complaint brought on by living in Crawley (a curious coincidence with the medical history of Rev. Sabine Baring-Gould). He may have found his source on that trip. Others claim that it was Bishop Jenner who found the Lisbon book. Whatever the truth, the source-text of Helmore's tune could not be found. Some even hinted that Helmore wrote the tune himself.

To get at the truth, we find ourselves in the excellent company of the eminent Cambridge-based plainsong scholar and nun, Mother Thomas More, aka Dr Mary Berry. In 1966, Dr Berry was on a research visit to France:

> My attention had been drawn to a small fifteenth century processional in the Paris Bibliothèque Nationale. It was

Franciscan in origin and probably intended for the use of nuns rather than friars. Turning the pages I discovered, on folio 89v ff, a number of troped verses for the funeral responsory *Libera me* in the form of a litany, beginning with the words 'Bone iesu, dulcis cunctis'. The melody of these tropes was none other than the tune of 'O come, O come Emmanuel'. It appeared in square notation on the left-hand page, and on the opposite page there was a second part that fitted exactly, like a mirror-image, in note-against-note harmony with the hymn-tune. The book would thus have been shared by two sisters, each singing her own part as they processed. So it would seem that this great Advent hymn-tune was not, in the first instance, associated with Advent at all, but with a funeral litany ... Perhaps it is a measure of Helmore's genius that he detected in this melody an appropriate Advent sound as well, one which conveys an unmistakable sense of solemn expectancy, not only for the Nativity of Christ, but also for his Second Coming ... Helmore was shrewd enough, also, to have been aware that an indubitable link exists between the theology of Advent and a procession marking the passage from death to eternal life.

It is just possible that Dr Berry was looking at the same book wheezily pored over by Neale. More likely, another copy of the same chant made its way across Europe, perhaps within the Franciscan community, and ended up in Lisbon. Either way, we have our tune.

We have, too, probably our most ancient carol. Next time you use it to invoke the great promise of Advent, you are doing so in phrases and cadences that may not have sounded entirely unfamiliar to the earliest Christian musicians of all.

'O Come, O Come Emmanuel'

O come, O come, Emma - nu-el, and ran-som cap-tive Is - ra-el

that mourns in lone-ly ex - ile here un-til the Son of God___ ap-pear.

Re-joice! Re-joice! Em-ma - nu-el shall come to thee, O Is - ra-el!

O come, Thou Rod of Jesse, free
Thine own from Satan's tyranny;
From depths of hell Thy people save,
And give them victory o'er the grave.
Refrain

O come, Thou Day-Spring, come and cheer
Our spirits by Thine advent here;
Disperse the gloomy clouds of night
And death's dark shadows put to flight!
Refrain

O come, Thou Key of David, come,
And open wide our heavenly home;
Make safe the way that leads on high,
And close the path to misery.
Refrain

O come, O come, Thou Lord of Might,
Who to Thy tribes on Sinai's height
In ancient times didst give the law
In cloud, and majesty, and awe.
Refrain

3

·: The Boar's Head Carol :·

riting in 1861, the pseudonymous carol collector and historian Joshua Sylvester divided traditional carols under six headings: legendary or narrative; religious (often by real poets like Southwell); 'numeral' carols; songs of the holly and ivy; boar's head carols; and 'festive' pieces such as wassails and drinking songs. It is a sensible and useful list (though when dealing with something so fluid and amorphous there is a good deal of overspill between and beyond his categories, and indeed with others, for example church anthems and school songs).

The fact that boar's head carols get a category to themselves testifies to their importance. The boar's head feast, with its music, runs through accounts of large-scale Christmas festivities from the earliest days. The humble turkey did not always have reason to feel nervous at Christmas.

Midwinter feasting, naturally enough, has always helped stave off the long British winter. Bones found at Stonehenge and elsewhere suggest large gatherings munching on pig and other delicacies. Later, romantically-minded scholar poets tried hard to link the boar's head festivals with various religious practices of the Vikings. One of the first, much-quoted accounts is of the occasion in June 1170 when Henry II appointed his young son to rule jointly with him. Holinshed (writing much later, of course) says 'king Henrie

The Boar's Head ceremony in Oxford in the nineteenth century

the father serued his sonne at the table as sewer, bringing vp the boars head with trumpets before it, according to the maner', implying a well-established ceremonial to go with the entry of the dish, complete with music.

Plantagenet and Tudor monarchs had the happy habit of giving members of their household a dinner as a reward for loyal service. The adult singers of the Chapel Royal, for example, were treated to an annual feast requiring one, or sometimes two, animals to be specially hunted in the royal parks at Hampton Court or the New Forest, though these were usually deer rather than boar.

Walter Scott, writing in 1808, has this account of a feast around the time of the Battle of Flodden in 1513:

> The fire, with well-dried logs supplied,
> Went roaring up the chimney wide: ...
> Then was brought in the lusty brawn,
> By old blue-coated serving-man;
> Then the grim boar's head frown'd on high,
> Crested with bays and rosemary ...
> Then came the merry maskers in,
> And carols roar'd with blithesome din;
> If unmelodious was the song,
> It was a hearty note, and strong.

Romanticised, certainly, but again showing the well-established details, musical and culinary, of the ceremony.

The carol itself first pokes its hairy tusks out of the undergrowth in 1521. Wynkyn de Worde was a printer, associate of Caxton, first literary coloniser of Fleet Street and St Paul's churchyard, and skilled entrepreneur servicing the newly expanding popular appetite for religious tracts, psalters, school grammars, Canterbury tales and books about love, saints and Robin Hood. In 1521, he published a short volume of 'Christmasse carolles'. Just one page of one copy survives, preserved in Oxford by an eighteenth-century antiquarian. It's the last page of the book, with two carols, one on each side. This is one of them:

Caput apri differo
Reddens laudes domino.

The bores heed in hande bring I
With garlans gay and rosemary
I pray you all synge merely
Qui estis in convivio.

The bores heed I understand
Is the thefe seruyce in this lande
Loke where euer it be sande
Servite cum cantico.

Be gladde lordes bothe more & lasse
For this hath ordeyned our stewarde
To chere you all this christmasse
The bores heed with mustarde.

Thus endeth the Christmasse carolles …

No music is printed: the technology to do this economically is still a few decades away.

Immediately, however, a complication arises. There is another source, also from the early sixteenth century and also preserved in Oxford, from a commonplace book owned by Richard Hill.

Here it is:

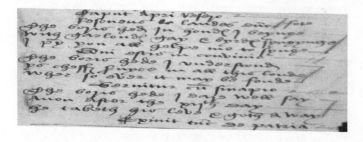

Tudor handwriting, cramped and crabby, takes a bit of getting used to, but this is what it says:

Caput apri refero,
Resonens laudes domino.

The boris hed in hondis I brynge
With garlondis gay & byrdie syngynge,
I pray you all, helpe me to synge,
Qui estis in conviuio.

The boris hede, I vnderstond,
Ys cheff seruyce in all this londe,
Wher so ever it may be fonde,
Seruitur cum sinapio.

The boris hede, I dare well say,
Anon after the xijth day,
He taketh his leve & goth a-way,
Exiuit tunc de patria.

It's clearly the same poem, but in a different version. The first two verses are similar in content and metre (although Wynkyn prints 'thefe' instead of 'chefe', apparently a typo), but the sources diverge markedly in verse three. Hill's version preserves the rhyme and metre of the first two verses, while Wynkyn's does something quite different:

Be gladde lordes bothe more & lasse
For this hath ordeyned our stewarde
To chere you all this christmasse
The bores heed with mustarde.

Hill's version could be sung to the same tune throughout; Wynkyn's needs something different for verse three. Perhaps there is a hint here of the shape of the accompanying musical ceremonial.

From here on, there are many accounts of the boar's head feast and its carol. Details differ, but the basic elements remain the same: the head is brought in on a dish, garlanded with silks, herbs and mustard, sometimes as the first dish of a gargantuan banquet. The words of the carol change considerably between versions, but there are always three verses, sung by a soloist leading a procession through the hall, stopping at three 'stations' for the choir (or the entire hall) to sing the chorus. Sometimes there are trumpets or other 'minstrels', in the procession or up in a gallery.

Here's one typical account, of a visit to Oxford by Henry, Prince of Wales, at Christmas 1607:

> The first messe was a Boar's Head, wch carried by ye tallest and lustiest of all ye Guard, ... next to him 2 Pages in tafatye sarcenet, each of y^em wth a messe of mustard; next to whome came hee y^t carried ye Boares-head crost wth a greene silke Scarfe, ... As y^ei entred ye Hall, He sange this Christmas Caroll, ye three last verses of euerie Staffe beinge repeated after him by ye whole companye:
>
> The Boare is dead,
> Loe, heare is his head ...

As he did with everything else to do with Oxford, the Restoration antiquarian Anthony à Wood got his hands on the story, noting in 1660 its antiquity and specific association with one Oxford college in particular:

> It must be remembered that at Queens Coll. Oxon. is every year a boars head provided by the manciple against Christmas-day. This boar's head, being boyld or roasted, is layd in a great charger covered with a garland of bays or laurell as broad at bottome as the brimmes of the charger. When the first course is served up in the refectory

on Christmas-day in the said College, the manciple brings the said Boars head from the kitchen up to the high table, accompanied with one of the Tabitters (Taberders) who lays his hand on the charger. The Taberder sings the aforesaid song, and when they come to the Chorus, all the members that are in the refectory joyne togeather and sing it.

This is an antient custome, as old as tis thought as the College it selfe; but no reason to be given for it.

Wood's text of the carol has gained the Latin line 'in Reginensi atrio'; 'in the royal hall', or 'in the hall of Queens (college)'.

The 'reason to be given' for the link with Queen's College lies in an 'antient' story which surfaced in print in the nineteenth century. It concerns a young scholar of Queens named John Copcot. Copcot was making his way through Shotover forest, to the east of the city, on his way to mass in Horspath church on Christmas Day 1376, amusing himself by reading Aristotle as he went, as undergraduates do, when suddenly he was confronted by a wild boar. Scholar and beast eyed each other. Then, according to an account printed in 1876, 'as quick as speech the taberdar thrust the volume, vellum, brass, and all, into the animal's throat, and then finished the business with the spear, whilst his opponent was digesting his classics'. An 1823 account gives the 'touching climax' to the story: 'Swallow that, if you can (cried the unarmed student, thrusting his Aristotle down the boar's throat). *Graecum est*, cried the boar, and expired, foaming at the mouth; for he found Aristotle (as many other throats had done and will do) too hard for him.' Horspath (where, incidentally, the lordship of the manor was once held by William

Byrd), has a window in its church commemorating Copcot and his quick-thinking escape.

And so the story, its carol and the ceremony march on through the centuries. Sometimes the boar's head is replaced with a wooden effigy, with a small dish of pitch burning under its nose, perhaps to represent the poor old boar foaming at the mouth. One eighteenth-century witness has the carol sung not to its stirring traditional tune but to psalm chants, which sounds a very dull way to do it.

Like the holly and ivy carols, there are many versions around the basic theme. Between them, however, Wynkyn, Hill, Wood and other early sources give us a more than usually authoritative early text. It is certainly our first printed carol, at least as far as the words are concerned, and indeed the first appearance in print of the phrase 'Christmasse carolles' attached to a seasonal poem for singing. The tradition continues, not just at its home in Oxford but in Cambridge, several English schools and, perhaps surprisingly, on American campuses. It's a good thing that it does. This song reminds us how much of our carol tradition is attached to older ideas of feasting and revelry as much as to Christian iconography.

There's something else here too. We no longer have to hunt and kill our Christmas lunch. But the boar was a formidable foe. Huge, sharp-fanged and dangerous, besting him was a mark of valour and skill. Richard III honoured him with a place on his coat of arms. When we buy our turkey, wrapped and gutted, we are, at some very basic level, celebrating the fact that we have tamed nature to our own convenience. It wasn't always like that. In the image of choristers carrying the head of a dead pig into supper, chanting ritually as they go, we are closer to the Lord of the Flies than to the Lord of the Dance.

Something primitive survives in our Christmas carols.

A boar, a boar, my kingdom for a boar …
Richard III's coat of arms, York Minster

'The Boar's Head Carol'

(solo)

The boar's head in hand bear I, be-decked with bays and rose-ma-ry, and I pray you, mas-ters, be mer-ry, Quod es-tis in con-vi-vi-o.

(full)

Ca-put a-pri de-fe-ro, red-dens lau-des Do-mi-no.

The boar's head, as I understand,
Is the rarest dish in all this land,
Which thus bedeck'd with a gay garland
Let us *servire cantico.*

Caput apri defero
Reddens laudes Domino

Our steward hath provided this
In honour of the King of Bliss;
Which, on this day to be served is
In Reginensi atrio.

Caput apri defero
Reddens laudes Domino

4

·: O, Christmas Tree :·

ecause they're part of a folk tradition, some carols can exist in different versions in different places at the same time. 'O, Christmas Tree' is better known today in America than in England. It got there with a little help from a family tree with many spreading branches of its own, including a Renaissance composer who lost his family in the Thirty Years' War, German students bellowing Latin songs into their beer, and a nineteenth-century poet and church organist. Among its cousins are an Irish revolutionary honoured by Lenin, the state of Maryland, Manchester United football club and the British Labour Party. Christmas carols have roots and offshoots in all sorts of unlikely places.

To some, 'O, Christmas Tree' may not count as a carol at all. The words are a translation of a German poem beginning 'O Tannenbaum', but a Tannenbaum isn't specifically a Christmas tree, it's just a fir tree. Apart from this bit of creative mistranslation, the poem makes no reference to Christmas at all, and certainly not to anything remotely connected with the Christian story. The tree is used as an image of reliability and changelessness in a fleeting world. Also, the poem's status as a translation shows perhaps more clearly than any other Christmas song how an oral, rather than a composed, tradition never settles into a final form.

Nobody knows what the 'correct' version is, because there isn't one.

The internet provides the perfect vehicle for revealing how this kind of dissemination by Chinese whispers works. Do a web search for the words of this song and you'll find, among much else, people looking for 'the words I knew in childhood', finding something a bit like what they remember but not quite, and asking if anyone out there knows the rest of the ones that go something like ...

> O Christmas Tree, O Christmas Tree
> How lovely are thy branches
> O Christmas Tree, O Christmas Tree
> How dum de dum dum dum dum
> La la la laaaa, in summertime
> La la la laaaa, in wintertime.
> O Christmas tree, etc.

Replies are many and various, but none quite matches the questioner's memory. The past is a foreign country: they do things differently there. Recorded versions have all sorts of different sets of lyrics. Versions by artists as potent as Aretha Franklin and Alvin and the Chipmunks are alike in their basic theme and their key features, but quite dissimilar in detail.

Does it matter? Not a bit. This is what an oral tradition is.

The tune, on the other hand, first appeared in print in 1824, with the name of a perfectly sensible composer attached. It, surely, must be safe from being mangled by the funny tricks of time, at least as far as important details like the number of beats in a bar are concerned? Well, no. Never mind whether the pairs of quavers are dotted or not, beneath the swooping strings and mooing horns under which this poor, innocent little melody is so often buried, you can find versions with four beats to the bar instead of three.

Should we be surprised? Should we be bothered? Not really. When something like a tune is passed on by memory and by performance, it will both change and stay the same. The same is true of language. That's how it evolves. 'Happy Birthday to You' started out in 4/4 time, and now it's in 3/4.

So, the version given at the end of this chapter is the tune as first published in 1824, to the harmony given in the Yale songbook, with one of the more common current English translations.

We pick up the story beneath a castle overlooking the river Itz, in Bavaria, in the dangerous days of the early seventeenth century, and the composer Melchior Franck. Franck lived through a period of musical transition. His huge output (600 motets and many other works) combines the old-fashioned sound world of Renaissance composers like Lassus with the new polychoral style brought over the mountains from Venice, and local experiments like fugue and 'basso continuo'. As well as his many 'learned' compositions, Franck also wrote songs. In one of them, he taps into an already well-established tradition in praising the humble and ubiquitous fir tree as an emblem of the natural world's comforting reliability and predictability, so unlike the world of men. And well he might. The area around Coburg, where he lived, was devastated by the violence and the political and economic degradation of the Thirty Years' War. Many musicians lost their livelihoods. Returning armies brought typhus to the streets. Franck's wife and two of his children died.

Franck's words begin 'Ach Tannebaum, ach Tannebaum, du bist ein edler Zweig! Du grünest uns den Winter, die lieben Sommerzeit'. The 'noble branch' stays green through summer and winter. Franck did not invent the idea of singing to a tree: versions of the lyric exist as far back as 1550, six decades earlier. His poem is not the beginning of the story, it's a staging-post.

Mediaeval German students liked singing Latin songs. Like most things students do, they were sometimes regarded with a degree of disapproval, as Brahms found to his cost when he incorporated 'Gaudeamus igitur' ('Let us therefore make merry') into his 'Academic Festival Overture', apparently not a very academic thing to do. One of these songs begins

> Lauriger Horatius, quam dixisti verum:
> Fugit Euro citius tempus edax rerum!

The laurelled Horace is hymned for his willingness to kiss the girl, drink the wine, defy the tyrant time slipping through his fingers and generally 'carpe' the 'diem'. No wonder cloistered academics find themselves dabbing feebly at a disapproving brow.

As usual, it is far from clear where this lyric comes from. It appears in print at the end of the eighteenth century, but it is impossible to be certain if it had been around for some time or had just been newly written. Naturally enough, the song then became a staple of student song books. It features regularly in editions of the celebrated 'Yale' song book from 1858. From there, having entered the US, it goes on to become associated with other words, including the State song 'Maryland, my Maryland'.

How did this tune get hitched to all these words, and what on earth has it all got to do with fir trees? Like the words, the tune is a creature with its origins in folk traditions and has passed through many hands and incarnations. It seems to first appear in print at the very end of the eighteenth century, to yet another German text, 'Es lebe Hock'. It appears without words in another printed collection at around the same time. Both appear to be based on the 'Lauriger Horatius' tune, which is itself probably a version of a Westphalian folk song. So, both tune and words are part of a process of evolution from hazy folk traditions into something approaching the form we know today. They first got together shortly after the tune first appeared in print.

Ernst Anschütz was a teacher, organist, poet and composer. He spent his whole life in Leipzig, plying his various trades there for fifty years. His poems were set as lieder, and he wrote the libretto for a singspiel by Carl Loewe as well as an account of the death of the soldier Johann Woyzeck, later turned into a play by Georg Büchner and thence into an opera by Alban Berg.

In 1824, Anschütz wrote and published a song, 'O Tannenbaum, o Tannenbaum, Wie treu sind deine Blätter!' with a tune that is a simple piano harmonisation of the familiar 'Lauriger Horatius' melody. The carol we know today is born. Sort of.

But we still can't quite claim that we have our author, still less our composer. Anschütz hadn't written the first verse, he had taken it from a version published just a few years earlier by August Zarnack, who, in turn, may well have based it on another version of the folk lyric, beginning

'O Dannebom', another name for the modest little fir tree. Zarnack had turned the imagery of the tree's constancy into a song about a faithless lover, which meant Anschütz had to edit its first verse slightly to fit with his second and third verses. Subsequent verses may not be by Anschütz either, though it's not clear who, if anyone, did write them. As is so often the case with these carols, Anschütz's role was to join together strands from all sorts of existing traditions. He did a good job. From here the song spreads its branches across the world with the growing popularity of the Christmas tree itself, famously popularised in England by another German import, Prince Albert.

During the rest of the nineteenth century, the song takes its hallowed place around the domestic Christmas hearth. The English novelist Maria Singleton wrote in 1865:

> Joyously did the little ones form a circle around that magic tree; and gleefully rang their voices as they saluted it in the well-known strains of that ancient song:

> O Christmas tree! O Christmas tree!
> How lovely are thy branches!

In 1879 John McElroy notes its popularity in America, calling the tune 'old, and a familiar one to all college students'. He gives part of a 'fine' translation by Longfellow, beginning 'Oh hemlock tree', and points out that the 'Oh Maryland' variant began as a rebel song before the Civil War. It is not the last time the tune is to be co-opted by the forces of violent revolution.

Irving Bacheller's 1911 novel *Keeping up with Lizzie* puts the tune to rather more peaceful use:

I was to dine with the Warburtons Christmas Eve, and be
Santa Claus for the children ... The little captain of three
years ran straight to Mrs. Bill an' lay hold of her gown, an'
partly hid himself in its folds, an' stood peekin' out at me
... She raised him in her arms an' held him close. A great
music-box in a corner began to play:
'O tannenbaum! O tannenbaum! wie grun sind deine
blaetter!'
　　Well, it was the night of my life.

Typically, printing lags behind oral transmission. English
versions of the song first appear in print in the first decade
of the twentieth century, after which it becomes a regular
feature of household song books and carol collections. In
1914, the song once again reaches out from Germany to the
English-speaking world in the famous Christmas truce of
that year, when, according to one soldier's diary, ' ... they all
began clapping; and then they struck up another favourite
of theirs, *"O Tannenbaum"*. And so it went on. First the
Germans would sing one of their carols and then we would
sing one of ours ...'

The tune has the memorable simplicity necessary for
lasting popularity: four lines, lines one, two and four all the
same (a feature of so many familiar tunes), line three a simple
downward sequence. Sing it once and you know it for ever.
Its opening rhythm makes it eminently suitable for singing
to all kinds of different words, as many budding wordsmiths
have noticed. Any three-syllable name with a 'tum-te-tum'
rhythm will do, from Field-Marshal von Hindenburg to the
Manchester United goalkeeper Edwin van der Sar: 'Oh, Van
der Sar, oh, Van der Sar, we'll always love you where you are.'

American place-names fit particularly well: 'Oh, Maryland, my Maryland'; or 'Florida'; or 'Albany'; or 'Michigan' … you get the idea. 'The Red Flag' is a revolutionary lyric by the Irish nationalist Jim Connell. Connell had wanted it sung to an old Jacobite tune, but it, too, got itself stuck to the 'Tannenbaum' tune, becoming the unofficial anthem of the British Labour Party, sung annually at its conference by such red-knuckled sons of toil as Tony Blair and Ed Miliband.

The image of green shoots in the depth of winter is older than Christianity. This song, like so many, taps into something all the more profound for being unfathomably ancient. It is part of who we are. Yet, like us, and like the imagery we use to describe ourselves to ourselves, it has changed continually, and changes still.

'O, Christmas Tree'

O Christmas Tree, O Christmas Tree,
What happiness befalls me
O Christmas Tree, O Christmas Tree,
What happiness befalls me
When oft at joyous Christmas-time
Your form inspires my song and rhyme.
O Christmas Tree, O Christmas Tree,
What happiness befalls me.

O Christmas Tree, O Christmas Tree,
Your boughs can teach a lesson
O Christmas Tree, O Christmas Tree,
Your boughs can teach a lesson
That constant faith and hope sublime
Lend strength and comfort through all time.
O Christmas Tree, O Christmas Tree,
Your boughs can teach a lesson.

5

·: The Holly and the Ivy :·

olly standeth in the hall fair to behold,
Ivy stands without the door; she is full sore
a-cold. (anon)

Deck the hall with boughs of holly. (Thomas
Oliphant, English version of words to a
Welsh New Year Carol)

Heigh ho! sing heigh ho! unto the green holly:
Most friendship is feigning, most loving mere folly:
Then, heigh ho! the holly!
This life is most jolly. (Shakespeare)

Now the holly bears a berry as red as the blood. (anon)

Green grow'th the holly
So doth the ivy
Though winter blasts blow never so high
Green grow'th the holly. (Henry VIII)

Down with the holly, ivy, all
Wherewith ye dress'd the Christmas hall. (Herrick)

In song, like in the garden, ivy gets everywhere. So doth the
holly.

The potency of the imagery is clear. The shiny green leaves and bright red berries brandish a powerful message of new life in the dark, midwinter wood. It's a short step to the image of the Christ-child. Throw in all the mentions of cherries and berries, mistletoe and yew, juniper and box, and our Christmas tradition really does become, as a Dutch carol has it, 'een hofken, er schoon bloemkens staen' ('a garden full of divers flowers').

The humble holly-bush and creeping ivy take their place among some of the oldest and strangest imagery in our collective lyrical memory, where the cycles of the natural world meet Christian ideas of birth, life and death. Here, too, are the three ravens paying court to the dead knight and the fallow doe 'As great with yong as she might goe', and the predatory falcon of the Corpus Christi Carol ('lully, lullay, the falcon hath borne my make away'). The eyes of these creatures still peer at us from under our not-quite-made bed of modern civilisation.

A recurring idea in the songs of the holly and the ivy is the competition between them for pre-eminence ('of all the trees that are in the wood, the holly bears the crown'; 'Nay ivy, nay, it shall not be, i-wys, Let holly have the mastery as the manner is'; 'the first tree in the greenwood, it was the holly'). Sometimes, this takes the form of a wooing song or mating ritual, the holly representing the boy, the ivy the girl (and the holly always comes out on top, from which we will avert our attention with some relief).

Their deep roots in this kind of imagery make these songs the perfect examples of how ancient, pagan ideas have become assimilated, though not fully absorbed, into Christian iconography. The church, naturally enough, has not always been happy about making house-room for superstition and secular merry-making. That favourite old celebrity St Nicholas, for example, carried all sorts of unwelcome associations in his sack; the Lords of Misrule, the ceremony of the Boy-Bishop and Twelfth Night Revels. All good fun, but definitely not text-book Christian practice. In London, on 5 December 1554, 'the which was saint Nicholas' eve, at evensong time, came a commandment that saint Nicholas should not go abroad, nor about. But, notwithstanding, there went about these St Nicholases, in divers parishes'. Folk traditions are as tenacious as ivy. Much later, Cecil Sharp is making the argument in reverse, defending traditional songs against incursions by Christians, and sticking up for 'the unconscious art of the peasant' before 'his carols suffered from the intrusion of theological doctrine'. Holly and ivy certainly received their share of such proselytising attentions, welcome or otherwise.

Some of these holly and ivy songs do not attempt to link their imagery to the Christian story at all. 'The contest of the holly and the ivy', for example, assigns various characteristics to each plant, or links them to some other species such as birds (the 'laverock' for the holly, the owl for the ivy). The masculine/feminine duality runs throughout:

> Holly and his merry men, they dancen and they sing;
> Ivy and her maidens, they weepen and they wring.

'The Holly and the Ivy' and its close cousin 'The Sans-Day Carol', by contrast, compare various aspects of Christ's life and ministry with some botanical peculiarity, often using a colour to symbolise the scriptural reference – red for Christ's blood, white for his burial shroud:

The holly bears a berry as red as any blood,
And Mary bore sweet Jesus Christ to do poor sinners
    good. ('The Holly and the Ivy')

Now the holly bears a berry as white as the milk,
And Mary bore Jesus who was wrapped up in silk. ('The
    Sans-Day Carol')

Verses, of course, vary between versions. A number appeared in print in the century or so from about 1810. Cecil Sharp got his version from Mrs Clayton of Chipping Camden, which he 'supplemented' with parts of a slightly different text sung by Mrs Wyatt of East Harptree in Somerset. Sharp also changed Mrs Clayton's 'obviously incorrect' last line of verse two ('On Christmas Day in the morn') to match the version printed by, among others, Stainer, Sylvester, and the Birmingham ballad seller Wadsworth.

Incorrect, or a local variant?

Thus do Sharp, Clayton, Wyatt and Wadsworth all serve their function as editors of the text we have today.

The refrain of this carol really needs to be considered separately. It doesn't quite fit. For one thing, the imagery suddenly takes a lurch inside. Up to now, we have been entirely out in the woods, among the bushes and briars. We stay there for the first two lines of the refrain, watching the sun rise and the deer run. Then, suddenly, we're in church, listening to an organ and a choir. It's an odd change of gear.

Also, an organ is a man-made thing. The word, in its meaning of a machine with pipes kept indoors, dates from the Middle Ages. The phrase 'merry organ' is used by Chaucer. Compared to the rest of the text, the reference is bizzarely modern. For all its relevance to holly, ivy, blood and thorns, our caroller might as well have told us he's switched on his iPod.

And it doesn't scan. The first two lines don't match the verses, and the last two lines don't match the first two lines. 'The playing of the merry organ' just won't fit the tune, whatever metrical and musical contortions ballad singers, editors and arrangers have put it through over the years.

It doesn't rhyme, either.

Is this refrain actually part of the same poem? Has it at some point been altered from a metrically unexceptionable but theologically unsound original?

There is probably a remnant here of an attempt to Christianise the lyric a little further than it really wanted to go. It's possible, also, that the refrain was appended at a later date to an existing poem, and that what we now know as verse one originally functioned as the refrain. This would explain the change of gear.

There is another line of inquiry.

Overleaf are two ballad broadsides. Both were printed in Birmingham in the second and third decades of the nineteenth century (the first may be the earlier). They are among the earliest printed sources of this carol.

Look carefully at the words of the refrain.

The second broadside (right) has 'the playing of the merry organ', as expected. The first (left) has 'the playing of the merry groan'.

The merry what?

Is this a mistake? Is it a coincidence that 'groan' is an anagram of 'organ'? Did a careless printer or feckless printer's lad, thinking about football or his girlfriend instead of concentrating on his job, muddle up the metal letters

The Holly & the Ivy.

THE holly and the ivy,
  Now are both well grown,
Of all the trees that are in the wood,
  The holly bears the crown.

  The rising of the sun,
  The running of the deer,
  The playing of the merry groan,
  Sweet singing in the choir.

The holly bears a blossom,
  As white as the lilly flower,
And Mary bore sweet Jesus Chrift'
  To be our Sweet Saviour.
                  The rifing, &c.

The holly bears a berry,
  As red as any blood;
And Mary bore sweet Jefus Chrift,
  To do poor finners good.
                  The rifing, &c.

The holly bears a prickle,
  As fharp as any thorn,
And Mary bore sweet Jefus Chrift,
  On Chriftmas day in the morn,
                  The rifing, &c.

The holly bears a bark,
  As bitter as any gall,
And Mary bore fweet Jefus Chrift,
  For to redeem us all.
                  The rising, &c.

The holly & the ivy,
  Now are well grown,
Of all the trees that are in the wood,
  The holly bears the crown.
                  The rifing, &c.

D Wrighton 86 Snow-Hill Birmingham.

THE Holly & Ivy.

The Holly and the Ivy,
  Now are both well grown,
Of all the trees that are in the wood,
  The holly bears the crown.

CHORUS.

  The rising of the sun,
  The running of the deer,
  The playing of the merry organ,
  Sweet singing in the choir.

The holly bears a blossom,
  As white as the lilly flower,
And Mary bore sweet Jesus Christ,
  To be our sweet Saviour.

The holly bears a berry,
  As red as any blood,
And Mary bore sweet Jesus Christ,
  To do poor sinners good.

The holly bears a prickle,
  As sharp as any thorn,
And Mary bore sweet Jesus Christ,
  On Christmas day in the morn.

The holly bears a bark,
  As bitter as any gall,
And Mary bore sweet Jesus Christ,
  For to redeem us all.

The Holly and the Ivy,
  Now are both well grown,
Of all the trees that are in the wood,
  The Holly bears the crown.

T. Bloomer, Printer, Birmingham.

as he hammered them into place, ready for inking? Was he dyslexic? Did someone proof-read it for him and get it wrong, an early instance of the curse of the spell-checker?

There is another possibility. 'Groan' might be correct. Is

it a musical instrument, a slang or vernacular term, perhaps, for some kind of bagpipe or 'drone', or a drum?

It's an immensely appealing theory. It makes the line scan perfectly. 'Groan' is a half-rhyme for 'sun' (perhaps more than half in Birmingham). And what a fabulous picture it conjures up: our carolling ancestor dancing round the holly-bush in the moonlight, swigging his ale, singing this song and playing the groan. It doesn't matter whether we have any idea what a 'groan' actually is or not. Just imagine it. Hear the sound of the merry groan. Good, isn't it?

The tune, unlike the words, has not undergone much metamorphosis. Apart from editors fiddling with the rhythms in an effort to get their particular choice of words to fit, the melody doesn't change between versions. It can't, really: it's a simple little thing. Hints of possible ways to sing it might be gleaned from the phrase-structure of the music itself: the distinctive rising major sixth in the first two lines makes it work particularly well as a round, sung at three beats' distance, like pealing bells (perhaps working best if the round stops after two lines of text). There are lots of rounds in folk music and children's songs. It's a great way to create instant harmony, and make a song last longer.

To take this idea a little further: the text of 'The Sans-Day Carol' is so similar to 'The Holly and the Ivy' that it almost, in some respects, sounds like a smartened-up version of the traditional original. Also, the two tunes can, almost, be sung together. Did one begin life as a sort of counter-melody or 'descant' to the other? Or an alternative 'answering' melody in a round? It would not be the only instance of such a process in English folk song.

There is one alternative tune to these words, completely

different in character, usually described as an 'Old French' melody. It appears in print a number of times between 1870 and 1930, including in Stainer's collection. It hasn't remained in use, however, perhaps because the French flavour of the tune does not really match the feel and rhythm of the words (and makes even less effort to accommodate the pesky spare syllable inserted by the merry organist).

If 'The Holly and the Ivy' has a theological point, it's less to do with the nativity than with what the nativity led on to. Not so much that 'Mary bore sweet Jesus Christ' but that he came 'to do poor sinners good'. Wedding these words solely to Christmas was always a marriage of convenience which never quite succeeded in covering up some basic differences between the two partners, though it's been going strong for a good while now.

And alongside the theology, of course, is a strong dose of the use of holly and ivy as decorations for the midwinter hall and home in the dark days around the solstice. Like the carol, the trees themselves look on towards Easter and spring:

> The holly hitherto did sway;
> Let box now domineer,
> Until the dancing Easter-day,
> Or Easter's eve appear.

'The Holly and the Ivy'

The holly bears a blossom as white as any flower,
And Mary bore sweet Jesus Christ to be our sweet saviour.
Refrain

The holly bears a berry as red as any blood,
And Mary bore sweet Jesus Christ to do poor sinners good.
Refrain

The holly bears a prickle as sharp as any thorn,
And Mary bore sweet Jesus Christ on Christmas Day in the morn.
Refrain

The holly bears a bark as bitter as any gall,
And Mary bore sweet Jesus Christ for to redeem us all.
Refrain

6

·: I Saw Three Ships :·

lenty of carols mix and match elements from all parts of the Christian story and none. Few give the mixture quite such an enthusiastic shake as this one. The results, when you look closely, are a little odd.

Our narrator watches ships sailing into Bethlehem, which is landlocked and twenty miles from the nearest river. There are three ships and two passengers. The adult Jesus never did enter into Bethlehem. Mary only did so before his birth.

It seems that, in this instance, several stories and aspects of stories have been piped aboard the good ship 'Carol' and sent sailing off round the musical world, picking up acquaintances and making friends among the indigenous population as they go. The associations of this song are rich and strange. Christ and his mother are compared to many things in mediaeval iconography: a shepherd, a pelican, a warrior; the sun, a pearl, the star of the sea. Sailors, not often. There are many layers of meaning beneath the sparkling surface of our seasonal sea-shanty, some sunk too deep for us to fathom now.

Our guides in these great waters are the men who wrote down and printed the song as it appeared to them.

The first is a seventeenth-century Scot called John Forbes. Forbes published his *Cantus, Songs and Fancies To Three, Four or Five Parts* in 'Aberdene' in 1666. He begins with an impressively thorough course in music theory, as taught by his friend Thomas Davidson at the local music-school ('Q. What is imperfect tyme? A. Two semi-briefs to the brief').

His contents show Scotland lagging some half a century behind the old enemy to the south in musical taste and accomplishment (no surprise, perhaps, given the events of recent decades). Here are songs by Dowland, Campion and Morley, ornaments of the Elizabethan and Jacobean court in London and long since dead. Restoration jollity has not reached Aberdene. There is one vigorously Scottish ploughing (or 'pleughing') song with its ritual naming of the beasts: Higgin and Habken, Hankin and Rankin, Philpie Foster and Macky Millar, Straboots, Tarboyes and Ganzel. Sacred and secular rub shoulders unremarked, as usual.

Then comes the song, reproduced overleaf.

The words repay reading with some care.

We begin with the sons of Adam, then a hymn to the Trinity. Then we hear the message of the angel at the

CANTUS. Three Voices.

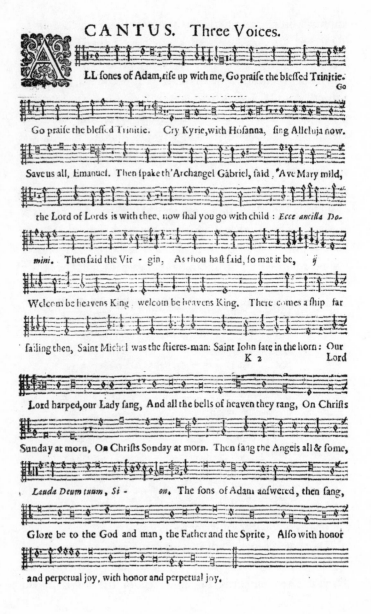

LL fones of Adam, rife up with me, Go praife the bleffed Trinitie. Go

Go praife the bleffed Trinitie. Cry Kyrie, with Hofanna, fing Alleluja now.

Save us all, Emanuel. Then fpake th'Archangel Gabriel, faid, *Ave Mary mild,

the Lord of Lords is with thee, now fhal you go with child : *Ecce ancilla Do-*

mini. Then faid the Vir - gin, As thou haft faid, fo mat it be, ij

Welcom be heavens King, welcom be heavens King. There comes a fhip far

failing then, Saint Michel was the ftieres-man: Saint Iohn fate in the horn: Our

K 2   Lord

Lord harped, our Lady fang, And all the bells of heaven they rang, On Chrifts

Sunday at morn, On Chrifts Sonday at morn. Then fang the Angels all & fome,

Lauda Deum tuum, Si - on. The fons of Adam anfwered, then fang,

Glore be to the God and man, the Father and the Sprite, Alfo with honor

and perpetual joy, with honor and perpetual joy.

Annunciation. Then, curiously, we're on board a ship, steered by the Archangel Michael, St John (the Evangelist, presumably) in the prow (or 'horn'), Christ playing the harp, Mary singing, bells ringing for a festival identified as 'Christ's Sunday' (a delicious phrase, with perhaps more resonance of Easter than Christmas). Angels sing. The sons of Adam answer.

It's a lovely poem. The rhyme-scheme is elegant and fluid. Lines and phrases are repeated at the ends of sections to gently emphasise the message of calm joy. The image of the ship takes its place in a shifting, kaleidoscopic overview of scenes from the lives of Christ and the saints. Liturgically, we are nowhere and everywhere: when would we sing Kyrie, Alleluia and Hosanna all at the same time? The figure of Christ appears first as a promise on the lips of the angel, then, without pause for breath, as a grown man playing the harp. Something similar happens in 'The Cherry-Tree Carol', too. Folk song meets liturgical ritual, with the usual results. A beautiful muddle.

The next source is much later, in 1833. In between, the lyric has lost some of its associations and gained some new ones. The two Archangels (whose festivals are part of the background hinterland of our Christmas celebrations) have gone ashore. In their place, we have picked up a first-person narrator.

Many carols use the first person plural ('Here we come a-wassailing'; 'We wish you a merry Christmas'; 'therefore we moun singen Deo Gracias'), betraying roots in the groups of carollers tramping from door to door in search of cheer, beer, cheese and sweeties. The singular form is more a thing of poems and lyrics of the fifteenth century and earlier, more suited to the solitary young man with just his lute for company, singing to the Virgin Mary ('I saw a maiden sitten and sing'; 'I cry to thee, thou hear to me'; 'Nay, ivy, nay, it shall not be i-wys'; 'I sing of a maiden that is makeless'). It's an unusual feature. Our singular narrator brings resonances from a number of traditions and legends to bear.

The editor of the 1833 source was William Sandys. He knew Forbes's text from a book of *Scotch Songs* compiled by a collector called Ritson, and quoted it in his introduction. He also knew several English variants of the carol, in addition to the one he printed.

There are lots. Many surfaced in the century after Sandys. The plot remains roughly the same: the narrator sits at his ease, watching as part of the Gospel narrative of Christmas unfolds before his lazy eyes. A common variant begins:

> As I sat on a sunny bank,
> A sunny bank,
> A sunny bank,
> As I sat on a sunny bank
> On Christmas Day in the morning.

Sometimes he sits 'under a sycamore tree', or 'at my cottage door'. An interesting plot-twist is that the itinerant mariners are often not Mary and Jesus, but Mary and Joseph. Sometimes we meet them on the way to the scene of the Nativity, Mary 'with child', sometimes on the way back, celebrating and giving thanks. In one, we watch from a Kentish cliff top as they sail up the English Channel. In another, also set in Kent or Sussex, they are on their way to be taxed. (In Dover? This transplanting of Gospel narrative to the green and pleasant fields of England is an interesting echo of the popular myth that Joseph of Arimathea brought Jesus himself to these islands, a story immortalised by Blake in his lyric 'And did those feet in ancient time/Walk upon England's mountains green', written at about the same time as Sandys assembled his book of carols. Shakespeare mentions it, too).

There are secular versions, too, appropriately enough from seafaring towns. Sir Cuthbert Sharpe, Collector of Customs at Sunderland and Newcastle-upon-Tyne, noted this (and its tune, a variant of our main melody) in the first part of the nineteenth century:

> I saw three ships come sailing in ...
> On New Year's Day in the morning.
>
> And what do you think was in them then? ...
> Three pretty girls were in them then.

Another change in the centuries between Forbes and Sandys is that the bells are now ringing on earth, not in heaven. Mary and Joseph join in, though they appear to have left Jesus's harp in Scotland:

> He did whistle, and she did sing,
> And all the bells on earth did ring.

A noisy carol, this one.

The story has absorbed another important influence, too. Forbes mentions only one ship. By the time Sandys writes the song down in 1833, there are three. A much-quoted explanation for this lies in the legend of the 'Kings of Cologne'. These mythical monarchs are none other than the magi, or wise men, who brought gifts to the infant Jesus.

Sir Thomas Browne, writing in 1646, tells us how they are supposed to have got to Germany: 'about three hundred years after (Christ), by Helena the Empress, their bodies were translated to Constantinople, thence by Eustatius into Milan, and at last, by Renatus the Bishop, into Cologne (1170), where they are believed at present to remain, their monuments shown unto strangers, and having lost their Arabian titles, are crowned Kings of Cologne'. Scripture, of course, nowhere says that the wise men were three in number, only that between them they brought three gifts. But legend (and Origen) has made them three, and given them names, and, as befits their status, they get a ship each. The townspeople line the banks of the Rhine, watching the stately progress of the sacred flotilla through their town, on its way to their enormous new cathedral ready to receive its consecrated cargo, prepared for the pilgrims who will pay homage to these brand-new antiques (and pay the inn-keepers and brothel-keepers of Cologne, too). Word spreads across Europe. The striking image of the three ships gets hitched to an English folk tune or country dance. Over time, through constant repetition and embellishment, the defunct wise men get shoved overboard, their place taken by members of the Holy Family in various combinations. Three ships, two passengers.

Forbes also mentions the Trinity. Is there a residual echo of this reference in the number of ships? The number three has many echoes.

Sandys's edition of this carol provided the principal source for most carol books since. His, therefore, is basically the version we have used ever since, and still do.

Here it is:

Notice anything odd? Sandys has chosen to notate the song in 3/4 time. It clearly isn't. It would be tempting to posit some learned theory about a coded reference to the number three and the 'bleffed Trinitie', the sort of thing a mathematically-minded mediaeval musician would have enjoyed squirrelling away in his scores for future generations to pore over.

Alas, the truth is probably more prosaic. Sandys wasn't a great musician. Some of his harmonies and bass-lines are noticeably clunky. Carol historian Erik Routley thinks his harmonisations sound like 'Auntie at the parlour piano'. Bar lines often don't go with word-stress. Look at his version of

The Cherry-Tree Carol ('Joseph was an old man'), which has an engaging wonky charm to its rhythm, and a big fat accent on the words 'an' and 'of'. And (whisper it not in Askelon), has anyone spotted the parallel fifths and octaves?

It's a mistake. No other edition follows his choice of time signature. Sandys hadn't read Forbes on the difference between 'perfect and imperfect tyme'.

In the decades after Sandys, many editors and compilers found this little thing irresistible, including Rimbault, Stainer and Terry. It became, or remained, immensely popular. William Henry Husk wrote in 1868 'it is found, under various forms, in nearly every collection of sheet carols'. The indispensable Cecil Sharp collected many versions, often of the 'As I sat on a sunny bank' variety. Louisa May Alcott quotes a rather sanitised version by the children's author Mary Mapes Dodge in a touching Christmas scene in her 1880 novel *Jack and Jill*:

> What shall little children bring
> On Christmas Day, on Christmas Day?
> What shall little children bring
> On Christmas Day in the morning?
>
> The grand old carols they shall sing
> On Christmas Day, on Christmas Day;
> With all their hearts, their offerings bring
> On Christmas Day in the morning

Sharp and others occasionally heard the carol sung to alternative tunes, as is to be expected, and one of these tunes made its way into a couple of published collections. But none ever seriously challenged Sandys's tune in the affections of carollers at large.

William Sandys preserved and recorded many of our best-loved carols. His editions placed them firmly and permanently in the popular consciousness. He probably wouldn't have passed Grade V theory, but without him, and his contemporaries and successors as collectors and compilers, Christmas would be quieter, not so tuneful, less rich in shared memory, and nothing like as much fun.

'I Saw Three Ships'

I saw three ships come sail - ing in, On Christ - mas Day, on Christ - mas Day, I saw three ships come sail - ing in, On Christ - mas Day in the mor - ning.

And what was in those ships all three?
On Christmas day, on Christmas day,
And what was in those ships all three?
On Christmas day in the morning.

Our Saviour Christ and his lady
On Christmas day, on Christmas day,
Our Saviour Christ and his lady,
On Christmas day in the morning.

Pray whither sailed those ships all three?
On Christmas day, on Christmas day,
Pray whither sailed those ships all three?
On Christmas day in the morning.

Oh, they sailed into Bethlehem,
On Christmas day, on Christmas day,
Oh, they sailed into Bethlehem,
On Christmas day in the morning.

And all the bells on earth shall ring,
On Christmas day, on Christmas day,
And all the bells on earth shall ring,
On Christmas day in the morning.

And all the Angels in Heaven shall sing,
On Christmas day, on Christmas day,
And all the Angels in Heaven shall sing,
On Christmas day in the morning.

And all the souls on earth shall sing,
On Christmas day, on Christmas day,
And all the souls on earth shall sing,
On Christmas day in the morning.

Then let us all rejoice, amain,
On Christmas day, on Christmas day,
Then let us all rejoice, amain,
On Christmas day in the morning.

7

·: O Little Town of Bethlehem :·

he hymn we know as 'O Little Town of Bethlehem' contains ingredients from two completely different traditions, mixed together by a representative of a third.

The words are by a nineteenth-century American bishop, Phillips Brooks. The tune is an English folk song. The credit for the idea of combining them belongs to one of England's greatest composers, Ralph Vaughan Williams, a man passionately committed to the musical history and traditions of his country, undertaking the entirely practical job of assembling a hymn book which people would actually want to use. He succeeded brilliantly.

Phillips Brooks was born in Massachusetts in 1836. He was sacked from his first job, remarking a little later 'my only ambition is to be a parish priest'. Ordained in 1860, his imposing character and gifts as a leader created many demands beyond ministry to his large and loyal congregations, most of which he turned down. He did, however, lecture at his *alma mater*, Harvard, and became Bishop of Massachusetts in 1891. When he died, little more than a year later, the city of Boston 'buried him like a king ... a great man had fallen in Israel'.

His monument is the church he built. Trinity Church is a true sermon in stone, its text the life and witness of a particular breed of late-nineteenth-century Anglican clergyman. Its massive, redbrick bulk roots it firmly in the history of the city clustered around it: the balcony where Sam Adams read the Declaration of Independence to his fellow citizens, the harbour which staged the Boston Tea Party, Boston Common, where Paul Revere mustered his ragbag troop, Bunker Hill, where patriots fought and died. The church itself drips with 'the beauty of holiness': the Venetian mosaics, windows by William Morris and Edward Burne-Jones, the first free-standing liturgical altar in the United States, choir stalls for the kind of 'thrilling music' he heard on a visit to Rome, and Brooks himself, six foot four of zealotry in stone, arm raised, Bible in hand, robes flowing behind him. Oxford comes to Boston.

Brooks could write. Listen to the rolling cadences of his funeral oration for Abraham Lincoln, delivered in a sonorous, patrician New England accent, yards from where Lincoln's body lay in Independence Hall, Philadelphia:

> One brave, reckless man came forth to cast himself, almost single-handed, with a hopeless hope, against the proud power that he hated, and trust to the influence of a soul marching on into the history of his countrymen to stir them to a vindication of the truth he loved: ... the swarthy multitudes came in, ragged, and tired, and hungry, and ignorant, but free forever from anything but the memorial scars of the fetters and the whip, singing rude songs in which the new triumph of freedom struggled and heaved below the sad melody that had been shaped for bondage ... But slavery will not die ... while one man counts another man his born inferior for the colour of his skin ... So let him lie here in our midst today ... this best and most

American of all Americans … May God make us worthy of
the memory of Abraham Lincoln!

This is the kind of preaching that echoes down the years into
the world of Martin Luther King and beyond. Thrilling stuff.

Like his English counterparts, Brooks was devoted to the
idea of congregational hymn singing. And his congregations
deserved the best he could give. Here, he experiments with
an unusual five-line scheme:

> The earth has grown old with its burden of care,
> But at Christmas it always is young,
> The heart of the jewel burns lustrous and fair,
> And its soul full of music breaks forth on the air,
> When the song of the Angels is sung.

This goes one line further:

> The silent stars are full of speech
> For who hath ears to hear;
> The winds are whispering each to each,
> The moon is calling to the beach,
> And stars their sacred lessons teach
> Of Faith, and Love, and Fear.

Brooks knew his Tennyson and his Matthew Arnold (and
perhaps the T. S. Eliot of 'Prufrock' knew his Brooks).

Brooks wrote carols for Easter, too. This one has the
seventeenth-century simplicity of the language which landed
with the *Mayflower*, just down the coast, the Puritan directness of Richard Baxter and the *Bay Psalm-Book*:

> God hath sent His Angels
> To the earth again,

Bringing joyful tidings
To the sons of men.

They who first at Christmas
Thronged the heavenly way,
Now beside the tomb-door
Sit on Easter-Day.

The most famous lyric in this collection is the first. Like the others, it is illustrated with a woodcut: a town, seen over the brow of a hill, its trees and sleepy church making it look perhaps a little more like Bethlehem, Pennsylvania than Bethlehem in Judaea. Brooks had visited the Holy Land shortly after Lincoln's death, and the peace he found there moved him deeply after the horror and bloodshed of the Civil War at home:

I remember standing in the old church in Bethlehem, close to the spot where Jesus was born, when the whole church was ringing hour after hour with splendid hymns of praise to God, how again and again it seemed as if I could hear voices I knew well, telling each other of the wonderful night of the Savior's birth ... for ever there will be a singing in my soul.

Like his other lyrics, 'O Little Town of Bethlehem' was meant for singing. Back home in Philadelphia, his church organist was a man who, as church organists often do, occupied his business in great commercial matters during the week, in this case real estate, only slipping on his organ shoes at the weekends. It seems that, on this occasion, Lewis Redner spent too much time on his business and not enough on his music. When Brooks asked him to set 'O Little Town of Bethlehem' to music, he did what composers always do when handed a deadline: nothing. Then, months later, the tune came to him in a dream on Christmas Eve, 1868. He hurriedly wrote it down next morning while shaving before church, and the children of his choir sang it for the very first time later in that Christmas season.

Redner's tune, 'St Louis', is the one often still sung today in the US. English carol singers use a tune with a very different story to tell. Brooks published 'O Little Town of Bethlehem' in 1891. In 1903, a decade after his death, it was included in *Christmas Songs and Easter Carols*. Around the same time, a raggle-taggle group of English eccentrics was tramping the lanes and villages of the British Isles, cycle-clips in hand, wax-disc-recording machine clutched bulkily under one arm, poking into pubs and church porches where old men and women sat puffing on pipes, thinking of the days before the railways came and remembering the songs they sang as the village lads marched away to see off Boney once and for all. Their visitors aimed to record this tradition before it was lost for ever in the brave new world of the twentieth century. They were a mixed bunch: Percy Grainger, brilliant Australian of exotic personal tastes, in Lincolnshire; Marjorie Kennedy-Fraser, braving the winds of the Western Isles of Scotland; Cecil Sharp (who signed himself C#), in Somerset; and, working on the music of the counties around London, two friends who had met at the Royal College of Music in London and wrote to each other as 'Dear V', 'Dear RVW'; Gustav von Holst and Ralph Vaughan Williams.

Vaughan Williams loved English folk song. It touched something deep inside him. When he first heard the song he calls 'Dives and Lazarus', he remarked: 'Here's something I have known all my life, only I didn't know it.' The melodies and modes of these songs, and their habit of evolving organically between one village and the next, permeated both his and Holst's musical philosophy (Holst's 'von' prudently dropped as German-sounding surnames became less socially desirable, a policy also adopted by the Royal family).

One sunny day in 1903, on one of his habitual field-trips collecting songs, Vaughan Williams found himself in the leafy lanes of Forest Green, Surrey, scribbling furiously as a knobbly old villager, Mr Garman, sang to him. As usual, other versions of the same song appear simultaneously elsewhere. Cecil Sharp collected this version in Hampshire at about the same time:

I am a ploughboy stout and strong
As ever drove a team;
And three years hence asleep in bed
I had a dreadful dream.
And as the dream has done me good,
I've got it put in rhyme:
That other boys might read and sing
My dream when they have time.

Me thought I drove my master's team,
With Dobbin, Ball and Star;
Before a stiff and handy plough,
As all my master's are:
But found the ground was baked so hard,
And more like brick than clay;
I could not cut my furrow clean,
Nor would my beasts obey.

The ploughboy whips and lashes his oxen, until

> The thunder roared from underground,
> The earth it seemed to gape:
> Blue flames broke forth, and in those flames
> A dire gigantic shape.
> 'Soon shall I call thee mine', it cried,
> With voice so dread and deep,
> That quivering like an aspen leaf
> I wakened from my sleep.

The mixture of a kind of didactic, sermonising morality with an almost pagan, pre-Christian imagery is typical of this kind of folk song. This was music to keep your ploughboy honest as well as keep him entertained. The tune is sturdy and strong, good for marching up and down a muddy field. Nice and easy to sing, too: four lines, all the same length, the music of lines one, two and four exactly the same, a vocal range of an octave plus a note, the highest note touched just once in the third line, the melody nicely shaped, made mostly of scale patterns, with no awkward leaps. Easy to learn, and easy to remember. Perfect for a large group of not particularly expert musicians to sing, and to enjoy singing. Vaughan Williams remembered these qualities when he undertook the job of musical editor of *The English Hymnal*, published in 1906.

Vaughan Williams liked giving congregations decent tunes, with proper harmony for choir and organ. He garnered good tunes for his book from anywhere he could find them: the psalters and hymns of early English Protestantism, Lutheran chorales, original melodies, and folk song. Not, however, the rather purple chromaticism of Redner's tune, distinctly American in flavour. Vaughan Williams preferred his choirs to sing the harmony of Bach and Tallis than indulge the 'debased' tastes of Victorians like Barnby and Stainer. For 'O Little Town of Bethlehem' he turned to the tune he had re-christened 'Forest Green', after the village where he had first heard it sung by Mr Garman.

It doesn't quite fit. Typically, Brooks varies his metrical scheme by inserting a seven-syllable line at line five: the tune has the more regular eight, six, eight, six, eight, six, eight, six shape known as 'double common' metre. This slightly spoils the effect of Brooks's rather subtle hint of metrical variety. But Vaughan Williams knew what he was doing. The tune scrubs up beautifully, brought in from the fields and wearing its polite new Sunday suit with impeccable modesty and manners. If you didn't know, you might almost never guess what a rackety upbringing it had. A triumph of the veneer of Victorian rectitude.

There are plenty of other tunes to these words. Most are congregational: some, like Joseph Barnby's 'Bethlehem', were written for these words; others, like Uzziah C. Burnap's 'Ephratah', were not. Walford Davies follows the German habit of adding a scriptural recitative before his charming melody, usually sung as a choir anthem rather than congregationally. At least one other folk tune, from Cornwall, has joined the shining throng. Needless to say, editors have found it necessary to fiddle around with Brooks's careful text: his line 'Son of the Undefiled' in the (usually omitted) fourth verse has become 'Son of the mother mild', which is a bit wet, and Edgar Pettman follows the practice of the first published version with music (but not Brooks's original published text) in reversing the order of the two halves of verse two, which is a bit odd (both work perfectly well). Like so many carols, this one is part of a tradition which is still evolving.

So next time these words and those notes work their familiar magic, remember the people who wove that magic for us: an American who imported peace from the Middle East; two dreamers – a naughty ploughboy and a real estate salesman; a devil in a puff of blue smoke; an English genius taking off his cycle-clips; and Mr Garman of Forest Green, Surrey.

'O Little Town of Bethlehem'

O morning stars, together
Proclaim the holy birth!
And praises sing to God the King,
And peace to men on earth.
For Christ is born of Mary
And gathered all above,
While mortals sleep the Angels keep
Their watch of wondering love.

How silently, how silently,
The wondrous gift is given;
So God imparts to human hearts
The blessings of His Heaven.
No ear may hear His coming,
But in this world of sin,
Where meek souls will receive Him still,
The dear Christ enters in.

O holy Child of Bethlehem,
Descend to us, we pray!
Cast out our sin and enter in,
Be born in us to-day.
We hear the Christmas angels,
The great glad tidings tell;
O come to us, abide with us,
Our Lord Emmanuel!

8

·: In dulci jubilo :·

he collector Joshua Sylvester helpfully categorised
traditional folk carols into six types. If we put all
our folk carols together as one group, we can
tentatively make a similar categorisation of our carol repertoire as a whole, at least as far as musical origins are
concerned. Such a list might look something like this: folk
carols; pre-Reformation liturgical music, including
plainsong; composed or 'art' songs; Protestant hymns and
psalms; tunes borrowed from instrumental and other repertoire; children's songs; secular 'party' songs; and German
chorales.

As with Sylvester's list, it's an inevitably leaky and
porous system of classification, with plenty of crossover and
sub-division. But a glance at the contents page of this book,
or at the pieces in your favourite carol book or service of
nine lessons, may perhaps suggest that it might help us to
discern some sort of order among the tangled branches of
our carol family and its ever-spreading and eternally evolving
diaspora.

German chorales are hymns. Just songs, really. They are
terrific for congregational singing, because that's what they
were designed for. Martin Luther was their principal, but not
their only begetter. Like Vaughan Williams and Sharp four
hundred years later, he and his successors were perfectly

·: 84 :·

happy to co-opt tunes from all over the place: folk songs, drinking songs, marching songs, lullabies, tunes by earlier composers and even Catholic plainsong, alongside their own original compositions. Anything, as long as it had a good tune.

Like the Catholic musical liturgy it replaced, the chorale repertoire has songs for each phase of the Christian year. This makes them a particularly useful resource at Christmas. The repertoire has given us familiar items at Advent ('Wachet auf' – 'Sion Hears the Watchmen Calling'); Christmas ('Quem pastores' – 'Jesus, Good Above All Other'); Epiphany ('Wie schön leuchtet der Morgenstern' – 'How Brightly Shines the Morning Star'), and everywhere in between. As usual, we happily help ourselves to the riches of another culture whenever it suits us.

One song stands representative of this repertoire here. 'In dulci jubilo' begins life with a charming legend attached. Heinrich Seuse (Henry Suso in anglicised form) was a four-teenth-century German monk. His writings are shot through with the idea of service derived from an equal love of God and man, and he developed for himself the title 'Diener der Ewigen Weisheit' – 'servant' (or, in some translations, 'servitor') 'of the eternal wisdom'. Like some of the earliest Christian mystics, he was much given to mortification of the flesh, and, like them, he was rewarded with many visions of God, saints and angels. An account of one appears in the (possibly autobiographical) 'Leben Seuses' (or 'Vita'), trans-lated here by Father Thomas Knox in 1865:

> There came to him a youth, who bore himself as if he were a heavenly musician sent to him by God; and with

Seuse in mid-vision: two near-contemporary images

the youth there came many other noble youths, in manner and bearing like the first, save only that he seemed to have some pre-eminence above the rest, as if he were a prince-angel. Now this same angel came up to the Servitor right blithely, and said that God had sent them down to him, to bring him heavenly joys amid his sufferings; adding that he must cast off all his sorrows from his mind and bear them company, and that he must also dance with them in heavenly fashion. Then they drew the Servitor by the hand into the dance, and the youth began a joyous ditty about the infant Jesus, which runs thus: 'In dulci jubilo', etc.

There is, of course, no tangible link between this account and the first appearance of the tune itself, in a German manuscript dated around 1400. But by the glory days of the Lutheran hymnal in the middle of the next century, it is clearly a well-established favourite. The tune appears in a number of such collections, the earliest extant example dating from 1533. A 1545 publication adds a new verse, possibly by Luther himself. The words are macaronic, alternating phrases in Latin and German, with the charming feature that the poet maintains the rhyme-scheme between languages:

> *In dulci jubilo*
> Nun singet und seid froh!

The writer even manages to switch languages in mid-sentence, keeping grammar and syntax intact and flowing seamlessly from one language to the other, thanks to the ingenious use of the linking word 'in', which works in both:

> Unsers Herzens Wonne
> Leit *in praesepio.*

Wordsmiths of the Reformation across Europe couldn't resist having a go in their own vernacular. A version appears in *Piae Cantiones ecclesiasticae velerum episcoporum* in 1582 with the words alternating macaronically between Latin and Swedish. Scotsman Robert Wedderburn included an English version in 'Ane compendious buik of Godly and spirituall sangis Collectit out of sundrye partes of the Scripture, with sundrye vther ballatis changeit out of prophaine sangis in godly sangis, for auoyding of Harlotrie', which contains lyrics by him and his two brothers and was published in 1567 (though all three Wedderburns died during the 1550s):

> *In dulci Jubilo,*
> Now lat vs sing with myrth and Jo
> Our hartis consolatioun lyis *in præsepio,*

And schynis as the Sone, *Matris in gremio,*
Alpha es et O, Alpha es et O.

Wedderburn's text is better than many of the later English versions. It's interesting that some of the best early writers of religious poetry in English were Scotsmen like the Wedderburns and their great predecessor, William Dunbar.

In dulci jubilo in Latin and Swedish, 1582,
maintaining the bilingual rhyme scheme.

From these beginnings the tune retained its place at the very heart of Lutheran music-making. There are harmonisations and elaborations by, among many others, Johann Walter, Hieronymous and Michael Praetorius and Dietrich

Buxtehude. J. S. Bach, for whom the chorale was the haemo-globin in his musical and theological bloodstream, used it a number of times.

Like so many others, the next stage in this carol's history is its encounter with inquisitively-minded English musicians in the nineteenth century. Robert Lucas Pearsall is something of an exception from the usual well-educated insider who shepherded our carols through the Victorian era. Born in Bristol to a Quaker army family, he trained and worked as a barrister, but had no formal musical or literary training. After his marriage and the birth of four children, the family emigrated to Germany where he separated from his wife, bought a ruined mediaeval castle in Switzerland and spent the rest of his life doing it up, living in rooms he built alongside and indulging his interest in the art and history of southern Germany and the Alps. When he died in 1856, he was buried in the castle's chapel.

Perhaps because of this highly individualistic approach to life, Pearsall's music has a definite stylistic signature of its own. His interest in Renaissance polyphony led to a real mastery of contrapuntal choral texture, particularly when writing in many parts. His madrigal 'Lay a Garland' is a fine synthesis of the melodic world of eighteenth-century glee composers like Samuel Webbe, with the techniques and preoccupations of the more melancholic madrigalists of Tudor England. Pearsall also wrote and translated some of his own texts, and his two sets of self-taught skills, musical and verbal, come together in his version of 'In dulci jubilo'.

It's a fine piece of work. His handling of the unusual texture of five solo and four choral vocal lines is masterly, and he wrings much expressive potential from his own version of the macaronic text and the stately triple-time dance rhythm of the melody.

Pearsall (the 'da' before his surname was added later by his daughter, in a Europeanising manoeuvre opposite to that made by Holst some decades later) gave us the version often sung by choirs today.

There are others. A version in the hymn book *Lyra Davidica* of 1708 gets rid of the Latin altogether. Another all-English rendering works from an early text which, in its turn, is entirely in German (and begins, confusingly, 'Nun singet und seid froh', which is the second line of the original macaronic lyric). John Mason Neale and Thomas Helmore produced a version, though, most unusually for them, they mis-read their source. They were working from the version printed in *Piae Cantiones*, given above. On the third system, the Swedish word 'ligger' has two syllables to the German and English one ('leit', 'lies'). Helmore read the two notes as 'double-longs', wheras they are in fact 'shorts' (in modern notation in 6/4 time, quavers instead of dotted minims). Neale gave the spurious long notes words: 'News! News!' in verse one. It's a bad mistake, and completely ruins the flow of the melody. Neale's text has become familiar as 'Good Christian Men, Rejoice', often with the offending phrase omitted. G. R. Woodward included his own translation (where he even managed to sneak in an extra Latin word, his little favourite '*io*', which Routley translates splendidly as 'Hurrah') in the *Cowley Carol Book*.

As usual, there are many versions, each subtly different, each seeking to translate something better, or translate it back, or modernise the spelling, or un-modernise the grammar to make it more like the Latin, or less like the

Latin, or take out the word 'men', or put it back in. The tune has become the province of pop and folk bands as well as early music ensembles and choirs of all kinds. Mike Oldfield took it to number four in the UK charts in January 1976.

Quite right, too. We're back with the dancing angels. Perhaps in some ways, Oldfield and those like him get closer to the hallucinatory spirit of Seuse's vision than surpliced choirboys do. Carols show off different bits of their genetic make-up as each generation discovers how to use them.

What this one brings to the modern choir stall and carol service is the faithful, earthy, determined love of singing which was the musical hallmark of the European Reformation and of one man above all other: Martin Luther.

'In dulci jubilo'

In dul - ci ju - bi - lo,___ Nun sin - get und sie froh!___

Un - sers Her - zens Won - ne Leit *in prae - se - pi - o,*___ Und

leuch - tet als die Son - ne *Ma - tris in gre - mi - o,*___

*Al - pha es et O!*___ *Al - pha es et O!*

O Jesu parvule
Nach dir ist mir so weh!
Tröst mir mein Gemüte
O puer optime
Durch alle deine Güte
O princeps gloriae.
Trahe me post te, Trahe me post te!

O Patris caritas!
O Nati lenitas!
Wir wären all verloren
Per nostra crimina
So hat er uns erworben
Coelorum gaudia
Eia, wären wir da, Eia, wären wir da!

Ubi sunt gaudia
Nirgend mehr denn da!
Da die Engel singen
Nova cantica,
Und die Schellen klingen
In regis curia.
Eia, wären wir da, Eia, wären wir da!

9

∴ O Come, All Ye Faithful ∴
(Adeste fideles)

f you asked a group of English carollers which item in their repertoire links Portugal, Benedictine monks and the Jacobite rebellion of 1745, would they say 'O Come, All Ye Faithful'?

Probably not.

From the earliest days of the Reformation, English Catholics sought sanctuary in continental Europe. One of the less notable among these exiles of conscience was John Francis Wade, the devout and musical son of a cloth merchant based in Leeds, who found himself caught up in the strong tide of anti-Catholic sentiment in the decades following the 'Glorious Revolution' of 1688. Wade fled to France in around 1731, aged about twenty. He found sanctuary first in Flanders and then at the Benedictine Abbey in Douai, not far from Paris, putting his liturgical knowledge and musical skills to good use as the monks' musical scribe and copyist.

Wade copied out the Latin hymn 'Adeste fideles' several times during the 1740s and 1750s. He included it in his neat, careful collections of devotional music, all good Catholic stuff, alongside hymns to the Virgin and prayers for the king. The 'Adeste' is a thing of great charm: four verses, a lilting melody in triple time, and a brief refrain, 'Venite adorate Dominum' (changed after the first edition to 'Venite adoremus Dominum').

It soon proved popular. In 1781, it was published in England in *An Essay or Instruction for Learning the Church Plainchant*, probably edited by Samuel Webbe and others. Ten years later, Webbe made a more extended arrangement of the tune and published it as number six ('Christmas Day') of his *Motets for the Year*. Both versions, and all subsequent editions, contain a notable alteration from Wade's original: the tune is now in four beats in a bar rather than three. Perhaps it was Webbe's idea. Thanks to him, we approach Bethlehem at the march, not the minuet.

The 1781 *Essay* is a teaching manual, full of practical information about scales, intervals and clefs (or 'cliffs', as it calls them), and the pros and cons of the four- and five-line stave. It is striking how many of our carol tunes began life in musical textbooks of this kind.

The *Essay* is also explicitly Catholic in content. Webbe was an important figure in the tentative rebirth of Catholic music in England, necessarily limited to private chapels such as the one attached to the Portuguese Embassy in Lincoln's Inn Fields, where he was organist. This was the only place in London where the Catholic liturgy could be celebrated. In 1795, the Duke of Leeds attended a service there and heard 'Adeste fideles'. He liked it so much that he commissioned another arrangement from Thomas Greatorex, composer, astronomer, organist of Westminster Abbey and later confidant of Bonnie Prince Charlie, and added this version to the programme for his 1797 season of 'Concerts of Ancient Music'.

From there, it found a ready place in musical soirées and society entertainments. The journal *Harmonicon* for 10 March 1824 included a review of a typically eclectic musical programme of, among much else, oboe concerti ('... Mr Ling has been practising since last season ...'), solo songs ('... warbled by Miss Stephens, with her usual success ...'), and this hymn: '... we should like, by the by, to know the name of the composer of this beautiful hymn: it is called Portuguese, and if the author be a native of Portugal, he need not be ashamed of owning it ...'

Many composers were suggested. The putative Portuguese link produced a parade of possibles, including the seventeenth-century 'Musician King' John IV, his son, and Marcos Antonio da Fonseca, also known as 'Portugal' (who was actually born twenty years after the first known source of the hymn). English candidates included Thomas Arne. Vincent Novello was said to have introduced it (Novello's daughter Mary Cowden Clarke said that he thought it was by the seventeenth-century English composer John Reading, which has no possible justification on stylistic or any other grounds). Handel was mentioned: the music does contain echoes of the triumphant, march-like style of other Handel-based hymns like 'Thine Be the Glory' or 'Joy to the World', but no suitable Handelian source comes to mind, and it seems highly unlikely that his music would have been sufficiently well known in France to be parodied in this way.

Confusion reigned. By 1825 the French composer Charles François Angelet could publish variations on the tune and call his piece 'Air portugais de Handel, varié pour le piano forte', thus neatly combining two popular attributions, both wrong.

Nobody mentioned Wade, despite the fact that the several copies which made it to England from Douai were all signed by him. That connection wasn't spotted until the twentieth century. Nor was an intriguing musical coincidence.

In 1744, just as Wade was working on his manuscript copies of the hymn at the monastery in Douai, the Opéra-cômique up the road in Paris put on a brand-new piece, all preposterous plot and thwarted desire. Presumably the monks didn't queue up to buy tickets, but the opera featured a tune called 'Air Anglois' which has remarkable similarities to the 'Adeste' melody. The coincidence of date and geography is striking.

Like the tune, the words set off around Europe without an author's name attached. Editors and compilers attributed them to more or less anyone they could think of, often, for no apparent reason, the thirteenth-century Saint Bonaventure. Then, at around the turn of the nineteenth century, the French Abbé, Étienne Jean François Borderies, decided to add three new Latin verses to take in more of the gospel Christmas story. Another (eighth) verse was added a few decades later by an unknown writer to include the 'magi', taking the hymn right through the whole Christmas season and up to the Epiphany.

English hymn writers couldn't resist the temptation of translating. The first English version dates from around 1797. A hymnologist writing in the 1890s knew of nearly forty versions. A century later the number had risen to at least fifty. The one that stuck first appeared in print in 1852.

Francis Oakeley was incumbent at the Margaret Street Chapel, Marylebone (later rechristened All Saints'), and a leading devotee of the Oxford Movement, following John Henry Newman to Rome and ending up as a canon of Westminster Cathedral. Rather conveniently for our purposes, Oakeley translated only the first four verses of 'Adeste fideles', the ones written by Wade. This is his first go at the opening:

O come, all ye faithful,
Joyfully triumphant

His many later versions add many small changes of detail.

The Latin of verses five to eight, by Borderies (and anon.), were subsequently translated into English by William Thomas Brooke, like Oakeley a convert, though this time into the Church of England (from the Baptists), rather than out of it. His four verses were published in 1885, inserted in the middle of Oakeley's to form a coherent chronological and scriptural narrative.

The hymn earned itself a place in the influential *English Hymnal* of 1906 (actually, two places: the four Wade/Oakeley verses appear on their own at number 28 in the 'Christmas' section, the longer 'Complete version', including the Borderies/Brooke verses, at number 614 as a 'processional'). The musical arrangement is approaching its modern form, too, with the familiar rousing pile-up of the voice parts in the refrain.

We have the hymn we know today. What we don't have is any real idea about who wrote it, where it came from, or how it got here. The pot bubbles with theories.

The 'Portuguese' association was around for a long time. There are various possible explanations. A modern Portuguese scholar states unambiguously that there were two copies of the 'hino de natal chamado Adeste Fidelis', ascribed to John IV of Portugal and dated 1640, in John's own library, lost in the Lisbon earthquake of 1750. Catherine of Braganza was John IV's daughter. When she married Charles II of England in 1662 she set up her own Catholic establishment, with music, in the Queen's Chapel in London. Samuel Pepys attended service there, and was much taken with both the music ('very good endeed') and the women ('my lady Castelmayne looks prettily in her nightclothes'), though not the liturgy ('frivolous'). Perhaps Catherine brought the 'Adeste' with her, a sort of musical memento of home and Daddy.

David Baldwin, Serjeant of the Vestry at the Chapel Royal, notes that from 1667 Catherine's household included a group of eleven Portuguese 'Franciscan Friars' (not Capucins, as Pepys wrongly identified them), who may themselves have imported or written the hymn. Baldwin thus evocatively invites us to 'picture the origin and first rendition of the "Adeste Fideles" amongst a group of friars each wearing a brown habit, hood and capuce with a seven decade rosary, a cord girdle, and sandals, singing in The Queen's Chapel'.

Or, perhaps the source of the Portuguese title is just a geographical coincidence. One of Wade's copies is known to have been made for the English College in Lisbon. Someone heard it there, found himself posted to the Embassy in London, and brought it with him. It's not the strangest itinerary in this book.

Alas, the most likely explanation is also the least romantic: the visit to the Embassy chapel one sunny Sunday morning in 1797 by the Duke of Leeds. Pity, really.

What is the original source of the music?

The alleged seventeenth-century origin can be safely discounted. It doesn't sound like anything else from the period, and certainly not like anything by John Reading, senior or junior, or John IV.

In 1910, the scholar and musical journalist G. E. P. Arkwright uncovered the 'Air' from the opera of 1744, and noticed its similarity to the 'Adeste'. He suggested that both tunes might be variants of some forgotten original, perhaps an English folk song (hence 'Air Anglois'). Thus, says Arkwright, 'a really fine tune (the 'Adeste') was compounded out of rather incongruous materials ... by some choirmaster (probably between *c.* 1740 and 1750), for the use of a Roman Catholic choir'. Uncannily, Arkwright has almost precisely described J. F. Wade without knowing of his existence. He has almost tripped over the truth while wandering in the historical shadows.

Others thought the 'Air Anglois' might be a deliberate parody of the hymn, named in ironical honour of its author, the serious-minded Englishman scribbling away in his cloister. That's how ballad-opera works: give your audience a comic version of a song they already know in a more serious form, just as John Gay was doing in London.

Another writer noticed that French hymn books of the nineteenth century used the opening line for a number of hymns for different seasons of the church year, like this Easter hymn:

> Adeste, fideles, laeti triumphantes,
> Inane sepulcrum conspicite
> (O come, all ye faithful, joyful and triumphant,
> Come and behold the empty tomb)

Perhaps there is an element of a conventional formula here, part of a common library of verbal gestures, without a single identifiable author.

Then, in the 1940s, Dom John Stéphan of the Benedictine Abbey at Buckfast, in Devon, published 'The Adeste Fideles: a study on its origin and development'. It's a first-rate piece of research. Stéphan had the happy knack of combining the most painstaking scholarship with a real enthusiasm for his subject and an engaging and readable style.

Stéphan identified six copies of the hymn from Wade's pen, the earliest (now lost) from around 1744 (later scholars have suggested a slightly earlier date). He dated his sources by comparing the versions of the words and careful examination of watermarks. The earliest book lacked a cover and, therefore, Wade's signature, but it is clear from comparisons with the other, signed, copies, that it is from the same hand.

Stéphan looked carefully not just at the physical sources but also their context and provenance. He noticed that the earliest copy contains a prayer for the king, with music, immediately before the 'Adeste'. This is a conventional enough gesture, with one striking detail: this particular prayer is for 'regem nostrum Jacobum': 'our King, James'. Catholics never recognised the overthrow of James II. To them, he remained the lawful king of England. When he died in 1701, he was succeeded by his son James Francis Edward. This prayer is for James III.

The potential link between this 'Jacobite' manuscript and revolutionary Catholicism in Britain intrigued Stéphan. He noted that several copies or records of performances turned up in Catholic enclaves within the British Isles, like Stonyhurst and St Mary's Priory, Dublin. Perhaps Wade's book, hymn, royal prayer and all, is part of the whipping-up of pro-Catholic sentiment at home in the period immediately before the '45 rebellion.

Modern scholars have gone further. Some claim that the words of the hymn itself are a clandestine appeal to English Catholics to support Bonnie Prince Charlie's insurrection, in the sort of under-the-bedclothes code which William

Byrd, another Catholic in internal exile, wove into his own music 150 years before and would have instantly recognised. 'Fideles' (the 'faithful') are Catholics. 'Bethlehem' is the true church in captivity (equivalent to Byrd and Tallis's 'Jerusalem'). 'Natum videte, regem angelorum' is a pun: Christ was born King of the Angels, but Charles Edward Stuart was born King of the English – Come and behold Him, 'regem Anglorum'. Wade added the instruction 'ad usum chori Anglorum' ('for the use of English choirs') to some of the surviving signed copies, not only confirming that these copies were intended for England but also, perhaps, inviting his readers to spot the pun. Not his joke, of course. Readers who knew their Bede, as Wade's surely did, would have recognised Pope Gregory's famous quip about the little blond English boys in the forum: 'non Angli, sed Angeli'. Wade, like Gregory, wants to get these 'Angli' back on the side of the 'Angeli', the Roman church.

Ingenious. But if it is a coded invitation to rebellion, it was too subtle for the stolid Hanoverian brain. Nobody noticed. The hymn was happily accepted into Georgian society. The Catholic call-to-arms became a Protestant tub-thumper. And both sides produced plenty of propaganda without resorting to Latin puns. As for the proximity of the 'royal prayer', Webbe's earliest English edition of the 'Adeste' places it alongside exactly the same musical prayer for the king, with the name changed to 'Georgium'. The copy which Wade sent to Portugal has the name 'Josephus'. It's a conventional gesture, of no great significance.

Stéphan also concluded that Wade wrote both words and music, though there is, in truth, no real evidence that he did. He certainly wrote it down, and in 3/4 time, in every copy he made. Why did later copyists and arrangers change it to 4/4? Is it better like that?

Many writers think so. They like the rousing march-like character of the version we sing today. But the lilting rhythm of Wade's first, triple-time, version is surely far more interesting, and certainly more varied. There's a lovely little cross-rhythm at the last 'Venite, adorate'. It is fluid, graceful, and irresistibly French.

Which creates another possibility. The tune carries distinct echoes of the character of the French 'Noël', such a quintessentially eighteenth-century creature, and its cousin, the folk song. It has the sequential refrain which is a feature of many such tunes, including the two in this book. It is also a little bit similar in musical outline to the royal prayer which precedes it, which also has a sequential refrain. Are both tunes (and the operatic 'Air Anglois') loose variants of some forgotten French folk song? Is there the still just-discernible twang of a rustic accent in the melody, which Wade and Webbe have not quite succeeded in scrubbing away?

If so, how did it turn into a Christmas carol?

Nice Christmassy words being bolted on to a familiar folk song is nothing new. Plenty of 'Noëls' were given prettified sacred texts by clerics during the eighteenth century, mostly in French, some in Latin, some in both. Something of the style of these texts can be caught in this extract from a lyric by the prolific French hymn writer Charles Coffin (who is still much sung in translation today), published in 1736:

Profunda noctis otia
Cœlestis abrumpit chorus;

Natumque festo carmine
Annuntiat terris Deum.

Specum sacratam pervigil
Dum turba pastorum subit,
Eamus, & castis pia
Cunis feramus oscula.

At quale nobis panditur
Intrantibus spectaculum!
Præsepe, fœnum, fasciæ,
Parens inops, infans puer.

(The heavenly choir shatters the darkness of night and
  announces the birth of God on earth in joyful song.
O come, let us go to where the crowd of shepherds
  gathers to keep watch around the holy cave, and
  bring our pure and pious devotions to his cradle.
See how this marvel is opened to us: the crib, the grass,
  the humble cloths, the mother mild, the baby boy.)

The words of 'Adeste, fideles' have something in common
with this style. Even the underlay of the Latin words seems
somehow French, much less heavily stressed than English
Latin would be (try singing 'Venite, adorate' as Wade wrote
it). Perhaps the first four Latin verses, like the last four, are
by some long-lost frilly French Abbé with a frilly French
name, set to a smartened-up version of some *chanson de
campagne*.

We don't really know. Lots of stories still swirl around
the possible origins of this hymn. As Stéphan comments
with a world-weary sigh, 'legends spread easily, though they
die slowly'.

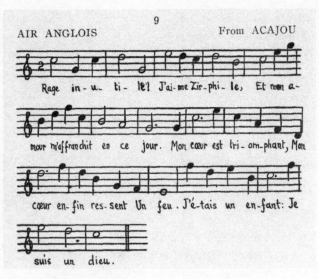

The 'Air Anglois', as copied by Arkwright, 1910

Whatever its origins or its politics, 'Adeste fideles' gives us something important. With its Anglicised offspring 'O Come, All Ye faithful', it takes us on a stirring stride through the liturgical meaning of the various acts and scenes of the story of the nativity, ending rousingly on Christmas Day itself: 'Yea, Lord, we greet thee'. It reeks of theology. This one is a genuinely ecclesiastical item. A hymn. It belongs in the choir stalls, and always has, whether or not the choir stalls in question were French, English, Portuguese, Protestant or Catholic.

O Come, All Ye Faithful

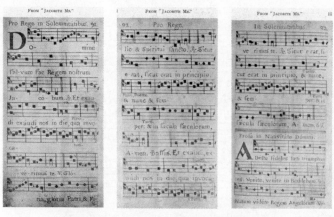

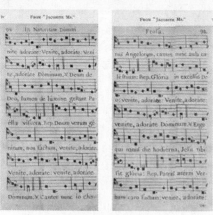

Pages 91–95 of Wade's 'Jacobite' ms (c. 1744 or 1740), now lost, as reproduced photographically by Stéphan in 1947, containing the 'royal prayer' (in two-part harmony) and the 'Adeste fideles' in 3/4 time (though Stéphan has not found it necessary to include the last line of the last refrain from page 96, presumably the same as all the other refrains).

'O Come, All Ye Faithful'

O come, all ye faith - ful, joy-ful and tri - um-phant, O come ye, O come ye to Beth - le-hem, Come and be - hold him, born the King of an - gels, O come, let us a - dore him, O come, let us a - dore him, O come, let us a - dore him,__ Christ__ the Lord.

God of God, Light of Light,
Lo! he abhors not the Virgin's womb;
Very God, Begotten not created.
Refrain

Sing, choirs of angels, Sing in exultation;
Sing, all ye citizens of heaven above!
Glory to God, In the highest;
Refrain

Yea, Lord, we greet Thee, Born this happy morning;
Jesu, to Thee be glory given;
Word of the Father, Now in flesh appearing.
Refrain

10

·: While Shepherds Watched :·

review of all the tunes and musical settings of 'While Shepherds Watched' would easily fill a book twice the length of this one.

It would be worth it. There are hundreds. The names alone conjure up the magic of place, people and association which these tunes evoke: 'Fern Bank', 'Tom's boy', 'Old Foster', 'Comfort', 'Liverpool', 'Leicester', 'Lyngham', 'Lloyd', 'Hail! Chime on', 'Morchard Bishop', 'Zadoc', 'St Cloud', 'Roadwater', 'Martinstown', 'Pentonville', 'Ford'; 'Bampton', 'Bolton', 'Bedford', 'Otford', 'Cambridge New', 'Canterbury', 'Cabyn', 'Carolina'; 'Adderley', 'Greetland', 'Christchurch' (or 'St Christchurch'), 'Redruth'. Some can only be partially identified: the 'Old Beer' tune, an 'old Ranter melody', a tune 'sung by the carollers at Barton-St-David', another 'from the Thomas Hardy family manuscript'. One is called simply 'Christmas'.

Their musical styles, too, allow glimpses into all sorts of corners of English life and its communal musical voice. Some have the sonorous, three-part harmony, tune doubled at the octave by tenors, which grew directly out of the old mediaeval technique of improvising a harmony around a familiar tune (when ordinary parish singers largely didn't sing from books because they couldn't afford them, couldn't read them, and had anyway known these tunes since before they didn't learn to read). Some have fancy little instrumental 'symphonies' and sturdy two-part fugues striding between melody and bass in the middle, in the West Gallery or Sacred Harp manner. Many are folk songs. Some are borrowed from other hymns. The 'Shropshire Funeral Hymn' is in a minor key, with the rich, modal harmonies and expressive shifts of chord reminiscent of Tallis.

Some versions, typically for carols, use a variant of the words. One or two add a refrain, like the splendid 'Sweet chiming bells', which instead of telling the shepherds to 'Fear not', wants them to 'cheer up, faithful shepherds, cheer up!', which is much more the sort of thing a sturdy English angel would have said under the circumstances.

As well as lending itself to all sorts of musical swaddling, the text is ripe for schoolyard parody. English readers of a certain age will remember versions from their own childhood, usually involving socks and changing channels on the TV. No doubt there are many others. One elderly singer recorded in the early 1970s has:

> While shepherds watched their peas and 'ops
> All boiling in the pot,
> A lone angel came fallin' down
> And spoiled the jolly lot.

The key to this hymn's enduring popularity must lie in its universality and its simplicity. It's about ordinary people and ordinary things: sheep, fields, men sitting on the ground about to tuck into their sandwiches and finding themselves caught up in a rather surprising bit of the Christmas story. It's engaging, characterful and full of joy. When we sing the Christmas story, the shepherds are us.

It tells its familiar tale in language which is simple and direct. There are no words longer than two syllables, and even those tend to be clear, expressive adjectives, adverbs and nouns, colouring in the narrative in bright, primary colours: 'mighty', 'meanly', 'troubled', 'glory'. Modernisers should take note: 'humankind' might tick certain boxes, but 'mankind' is shorter. (And it's what the man wrote.)

It's impossible, then, to attempt here anything approaching a comprehensive review of the history of this unassuming little gem. A closer look at just two of its many musical incarnations will pretty much tell the entire history of congregational singing in England.

The story begins in the very earliest days of the Reformation. Christopher Tye was a fine composer for the old Latin rite of the pre-Reformation Catholic church. Unlike some of his contemporaries, he was also an enthusiastic Protestant. When Edward VI came to the throne in 1547, Tye embraced the opportunities for musical innovation presented by the devout, reformist boy-King. Edward wanted his words in English, and his music simple enough not to get in the way of the words. Tye responded with a metrical version of 'The Actes of the Apostles', set to his own music, four parts, little repetition, no drawing-out of words for musical effect. The idea was that moralising little devotional verses of this kind could be sung at home, by anybody, for entertainment and spiritual enlightenment, and they were enormously popular. Literary quality, unfortunately, did not always keep up with popularity. Tye was no Thomas Cranmer:

Which sayd, ye men of Galilee
Why gaze ye up in bayne:

> Thys Jesus thus, up take from us
> Shal thus come downe agayne.

Routley describes Tye's verses as 'from the literary point of view pure *Stuffed Owl* from end to end'.

Notwithstanding his rather clunky versifying, for our purposes the interest of Tye's 'Actes' lies in the 'meane' (top) part of the second half of his setting of chapter VIII, which goes:

Try singing it from 'And through the regions crept' (note that middle C is on the lowest line of the stave). Sound familiar?

The story now proceeds with the progress of popular psalm singing through the reign of Elizabeth I and beyond. Tye arranged his verses in 'common metre', that is, four-line stanzas in a pattern of eight, six, eight, six syllables. The vast majority of the vast number of versions of the psalms produced at this time used this same metre. Any psalm could be sung to any tune in the same metrical pattern. The practice of mixing and matching text and melody, such a creative and confusing a part of this history, was born. At the same time, bits of tunes could migrate from one setting to another, or sometimes two could be sung at once if their harmonies matched (or even if they didn't, quite). Congregations, and, no less importantly, families, could sing their favourite psalms to tunes they already knew and liked: 'the one whose sense suits "Mount Ephraim"', as Thomas Hardy later put it, or the one which Dad knows the chords to on the theorbo, or the kids can manage on the household chest of viols.

The *Whole Booke of Psalmes*, begun in Edward's reign, went through many hundreds of printings in the following century-and-a-half, gathering well-known tunes like 'Ein feste burg' as it went. Queen Elizabeth allowed 'an hymn' (meaning a psalm) to be sung 'before and after' (but not during) the actual service, but their content was strictly limited to the items in the *Whole Booke*: canticles, creed, Lord's Prayer, psalms and one or two other suitable texts. But no Christmas carols. Certainly not. To the new breed of Puritan parson, our semi-pagan country cousins are still a thing for the churchyard, not the church.

The ongoing popularity of psalm singing presented considerable opportunities to the musical entrepreneur. Thomas East was a printer, and in 1592 he issued a psalter. As usual, he shuffled the pack of tunes and texts to meet his market, and included a number of tunes not seen before in print. One of them, by the curious process of cross-referencing and borrowings familiar to anyone who has dabbled in folk traditions, is based on Tye's meane part of forty years before, tune in the tenor, as was customary. East also continued the slightly eccentric habit of the English psalter-makers of naming their tunes after a favourite place, or some other reference entirely unconnected with its text. He called this one 'Winchester' (later re-christened 'Winchester Old' when someone decided to use the name 'Winchester New' for the tune to the Advent hymn 'On Jordan's Bank the Baptist's Cry').

In 1696, a new psalm book eventually arrived to supersede the old one. The new text, printed without tunes, was by Nicholas Brady and the Poet Laureate, Nahum Tate. Their book was quickly followed by a supplement, in which they allowed themselves one, just one, Christmas hymn, which they called 'Song of the Angels at the Nativity of our Blessed Saviour'. Like Tye before them, they adopted the time-honoured practice of putting a suitable section of the biblical narrative into a nice, manageable metrical scheme, for easy, practical singing to a familiar tune, the parish clerk bellowing out each line for the congregation to repeat in a technique known as 'lining-out' (a splendidly practical bit of communal music-making which has the added advantage of saving money on books). The poem, 'Whilst Shepherds Watched their Flocks by Night', is usually ascribed to Tate, and it was the only Christmas carol which could legally be sung in English churches for most of the rest of the eighteenth century, which is at least partly why it caught on quite as spectacularly as it did.

Another reason is Tate and Brady's instinctive genius for simplicity. Many carols have been fiddled around with by subsequent editors and arrangers. Not this one. It doesn't need it. Apart from their first word, which has perhaps permissibly elided from their 'whilst' to the slightly less sibilant 'while' over the years, this is the very first English carol which we still sing in the version in which its authors wrote it. Three hundred years and counting. Tate and Brady's cheery little message of goodwill really does look as if it might begin and never cease.

Through its roots in the psalm traditions of the sixteenth to the early eighteenth centuries, 'While Shepherds Watched' really does tell, all by itself, the story of a particular strand of the history of congregational singing in England. By their master-stroke of setting their text in a simple, well-known metre, its authors allowed it to spread its wings through the later eighteenth and nineteenth centuries and on into the twentieth, forming local alliances with favourite tunes in virtually every village, church, non-conformist chapel, brass band and fireside snug in England. The results are rich, varied, personal and deeply moving. Just one will have to stand representative here.

Thomas Clark was a Canterbury cobbler. In 1805 he published *A Sett of Psalm & Hymn Tunes with some Select Pieces and an Anthem*, including an irresistibly jolly melody in 'common' metre (with the last two lines repeated), which he set to the hymn 'Grace 'tis a charming sound'. By the usual process of singers cheerfully nicking a tune to sing to different words with the same metre, his melody soon found itself attached to Tate's lyric 'While Shepherds Watched', and in this incarnation it gained widespread use, including in Dorset and the West country, which it has steadfastly hung on to more or less ever since. Clark spent much of his long life making music in parish churches and Sunday schools around Canterbury, and his tune bears the name of a pretty little town on the A229 between Maidstone and Hastings, where, perhaps, he wrote it one shady afternoon under the flinty bulk of the old church, the scent of hops wafting gently across the Weald, or taught it one Sunday morning to the children of the parish, accompanied by their uncles and cousins on serpents, clarinets and harmoniums. The tune, and the town, are called Cranbrook.

Oddly, this tune, with its roots in the hop-fields of Kent, has ended up as the unofficial 'national' anthem of Yorkshire. Some fifty years after Clark wrote his melody, the members of Halifax parish church choir were on a day out to Ilkley moor. As singers do, they whiled away the journey by singing their own (not very religious) words to their favourite hymn tunes. The story goes that they improvised a lyric about a man who chose to woo his girlfriend out on the moor without taking the obvious precaution of wearing a hat, leading indirectly to their both being eaten by ducks. The song, in the local dialect, is 'On Ilkla moor baht 'at', a curious example of a 'folk song' appearing to evolve from a composed song rather than the other way round.

It's one detail in the history of one song. On its own, it barely even hints at the extent of the melodic peregrinations of this carol around England, a sort of musical Mr Pickwick, picking up friends as it goes. It met its long-term partner, the tune 'Winchester', probably in the nineteenth century. In America it hooked up with an arrangement of an operatic number by Handel.

But the full richness and variety of its history will, like the shepherds, have to wait.

'While Shepherds Watched'

'Cranbrook'

Whilst shep-herds watched their flocks by night, All sea - ted__ on__ the__ ground,

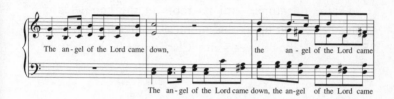

The an-gel of the Lord came down, the an-gel of the Lord came

The an-gel of the Lord came down, the an-gel of the Lord came

And glo - ry shone a - round, and glo-ry shone a -

down, And glo-ry shone a - round, and

down, And glo - ry shone a - round, and glo - ry shone a -

round, and glo - ry shone a - round.

glo-ry shone a - round, and glo - ry shone a - round.

round, and glo - ry shone a - round.

'Winchester Old'

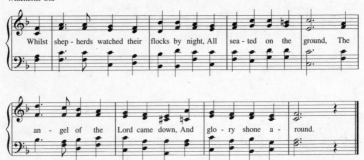

Whilst shep-herds watched their flocks by night, All sea-ted on the ground, The an-gel of the Lord came down, And glo-ry shone a-round.

'Fear not!' said he, for mighty dread
Had seized their troubled mind;
'Glad tidings of great joy I bring
To you and all mankind.

'To you, in David's town, this day
Is born of David's line
The Saviour, who is Christ the Lord,
And this shall be the sign:

'The heav'nly Babe you there shall find
To human view displayed,
All meanly wrapped in swathing bands,
And in a manger laid.'

Thus spake the seraph and forthwith
Appeared a shining throng
Of angels praising God, and thus
Address their joyful song:

'All glory be to God on high,
And to the Earth be peace;
Good will henceforth from heav'n to men
Begin and never cease!'

11

∵ The Fleecy Care ∴

arols are a body of songs which everybody knows. Within that corpus, some carols can have many local variants. Some of those variants can be seen as genuinely separate items in their own right.

'The Fleecy Care' is clearly a version of 'While Shepherds Watched'. It is, however, also right and proper to consider it as a discrete piece, mainly because it has eight syllables to each of its four lines instead of the eight, six, eight, six 'common' metre of 'While Shepherds Watched', and can't therefore be sung to any of the host of tunes associated with Tate and Brady's original. In both words and music, this is a different song. And it's a beauty.

The secret appears to lie buried somewhere in eighteenth-century Warwickshire.

Roy Palmer, along with Bob and Jacqueline Patten, Reg Hall, Bob Copper, Keith Summers, Steve Roud and others, have continued the task begun by Vaughan Williams, Cecil Sharp and A. L. Lloyd in collecting folk songs from all round the country. They are among the heroes of English music, and the fruits of their garnerings, held mainly by the English Folk Dance and Song Society at the appropriately named Cecil Sharp House in Chalk Farm, Camden, and in the British Library's sound archive, are a limitless treasure-house of local genius.

Palmer found 'The Fleecy Care' in Napton, in Shake-speare country. He has this to say about it: 'Many villages have carols which they claim as their own. In some cases, these are local variants of standard items; in others, survivors from now-forgotten hymnals; and occasionally, genuinely unique. This one ... comes, I believe, into the last category.'

The eighteenth-century connection can be found in another part of Warwickshire, just twenty-five miles or so from Napton, in Nuneaton.

Joseph Key was an exciseman by profession, and one of the army of well-educated, highly practical, amateur musicians who brought something of the academic, 'learned' style of music-making to the parish choir and village band as they gathered in the west gallery of their local church every Sunday. Key died in 1784, and just a year later a collection of his compositions was issued by a London publisher. The contents page gives a pretty good feel of the musical reach of a medium-sized, provincial parish church in a prosperous market town like Nuneaton: *Five Anthems, Four Collects, Twenty Psalm Tunes*. At one end of the scale of musical elabo-ration, the anthems are artful little things, designed to be performed with a small group of instruments, with elegant 'symphonies' in the Handel style, and tuneful solo sections for the parish's most accomplished singers, the rank-and-file members of the choir no doubt peering jealously from behind their copies, waiting for the chorus at the end and wondering why they weren't picked to do the solo.

At the other extreme, Key's 'psalm tunes' are in the direct line of Protestant music-making dating back to the sixteenth century, a tradition which by this date had descended into dullness. All the music celebrates the principle of inclusivity, of joining in, which has been such an important feature of the philosophy and practice of Protestant music since Luther. And, like Luther, one of the ways you can involve ordinary people into your musical worship is by using tunes they already know: folk songs.

Key's anthem 'As Shepherds Watched their Fleecy Care' uses the same melody as the folk tune collected by Roy Palmer in nearby Napton two centuries later. In the approved Handelian manner, Key begins with the tune sung more or less straight by his soprano soloist, then turns it into something rather more elaborate. But it's unmistakably the same tune. The inference is that this tune, and these words, are a genuine local vernacular variant which found its way into the shared folk memory of both Joseph Key and of his musical descendant who sang it to Roy Palmer, perhaps filtered through one of Palmer's 'forgotten hymnals' on the way. There is a slightly self-conscious artfulness to the words, so perhaps there is the hand of a real poet hovering over them somewhere. Who knows?

Whatever its genesis, this song has a gorgeous, lilting quality, the repeated last line giving the tune a charmingly lopsided five-line shape, the final arrival back at the key-note teasingly delayed by the half-close at the end of the last line of text, resolved in the repetition. It is, at the same time, both a fascinating insight into an intensely local version of pastoral, and a thing of beauty in its own right.

'The Fleecy Care'

While shep-herds watched their flee-cy care A heav-'nly an-gel did ap-pear,
"Shep-herds, at-tend, to you I bring Glad ti-dings of a
new-born king, glad ti-dings of a new-born king."

In Bethlehem's town this blessed morn
A Saviour of mankind is born,
Born of a spotless virgin pure,
Free from all sin and guile secure.

In swaddling clothes this babe behold,
No costly garb his limbs enfold,
Laid in a manger, there you will find
The great redeemer of mankind.

Arise, your tender care forsake,
With hasty steps your journey take
To David's city, there you will see
The pattern of humanity.

To save us from eternal death
The great Messiah came to earth.
Then let us with united voice
Sing Alleluia, all rejoice'.

12

·: Ding dong! Merrily on High :·

n 1589 a manual of courtly dance was published by the Frenchman Thoinot Arbeau. That isn't his real name. He was actually a priest called Jehan Tabourot. 'Thoinot Arbeau' is a pen-name and an anagram of his real name (though the anagram doesn't quite work in modern spelling: you have to read 'i' and 'j' as the same letter, Latin-style).

His book is called *Orchésographie*. Like so many of the productions of the new commercial presses across Europe, it is a thing of beauty, lavishly illustrated, carefully type-set on the page, with a gorgeous title page, florid dedication, and handsome initial letters draped in foliage and classical deities. His course of instruction in how to 'apprendre a dancer' and 'battre le Tambour' is set out in the form of a dialogue between teacher and student, the approved method derived from Socrates and much used at the time, for example by Thomas Morley and our Scots friend John Forbes in their textbooks of music theory. The teacher is the pseudonymous author Arbeau, the pupil a young man called Capriol.

It's a charming and extremely interesting book. It tells you how to tie and carry a large drum (and a sword), and what different national styles of drumming are like, and gives extensive and detailed information about all sorts of dances, complete with woodcuts of a rather self-conscious young couple in full fig doing the 'sault majeur' and the 'pieds en l'air'.

There is a great deal of music, painstakingly set up in movable type, beautifully clear. There are drum rhythms, plenty of tunes for fife and flute, and a gorgeous little love song for voices in four parts. Above all, there are 'airs': dance-tunes.

Arbeau classifies these according to the type of dance: the 'courante', the 'basse-dance', the 'gaillarde'. Within these classifications, many of the tunes have names: 'Air de la gaillarde appellee Anthoinette', 'Branle de Poictou'. Some of the names imply a foreign origin: the 'Pavane d'Espagne' and the 'Air de la gaillarde appelle *La traditore my fa morire*'.

Peter Warlock made memorable use of these melodies in his 'Capriol Suite' for strings. Stravinsky drew on these resources too, in his ballet *Agon*, with somewhat spikier results. They're folk tunes. The publication brings together a wealth of tunes bursting with what Cecil Sharp would have recognised as the 'unconscious art' of the folk musician, very like its almost exact contemporary *Piae Cantiones*. It's wonderful stuff. There are many more riches waiting to be mined here.

Towards the end of the book Arbeau sets out his detailed dance steps alongside the melodies which go with them. This gives him an interesting problem: how to present the dance steps, which need to be read top-to-bottom, in proper alignment with the matching notes and beats of the music, which is read left-to-right. He comes up with an ingenious solution: put the musical stave vertically down the side of the page with the steps alongside:

Brilliant.

Among his last dances are a set of the type known as the 'branle' (the 'branle d'Escosse', the 'branle des Pois', the 'branle couppé nõmé Cassandre'), each with its own detailed directions for dancing – as explained in an exchange between our young pupil and a by now apparently rather exasperated teacher:

Capriol: Comment danciez vous ces branles que vous dictes?
Arbeau: Vous le verrez par leur tabulature.

Right at the end is a florid little melody, stretching vertically over two pages, with the grand-sounding name 'Branle de l'Official'.

The story now moves on 300 years and 400 miles north, into familiar *curriculum vitae* territory for the English carol. A folk tune of indeterminate origin, nothing whatever to do with Christmas, is discovered in an old book by an English clergyman, who adds words in a suitably old-fashioned style, publishes it in a carol book, and thus places it smack in the middle of our Christmas carol repertoire as if it had been there all its life, where it has stayed ever since.

George Ratcliffe Woodward belongs firmly in the tradition of idealistic, high-church Anglican priests, scholars and hymn writers who feature so strongly in this story. He served his ministry at St Barnabas', Pimlico, and at Little Walsingham in Norfolk, where he would sometimes play the euphonium in procession through the ruined abbey gateway and along the muddy edges of the turnip fields to the shrine (the Anglican one, of course). Like Baring-Gould he wrote voluminously about saints and legends, and published books of poems. Like the earlier great partnership of Helmore and Neale he was fascinated by plainsong, Renaissance music and the traditions of orthodox Christianity. Like them, too, he was part of a creative double-act with a long-term musical collaborator, his Cambridge friend and fellow Caian, Charles Wood. Between them, their many books of Christmas music represent, alongside Sharp, the most important contributions to the repertoire between Helmore and Neale and the later work of Vaughan Williams, Percy Dearmer and Martin Shaw.

'Ding dong! Merrily on High' first appeared in the *Cambridge Carol-Book* in 1924. The words are by Woodward, the tune is Arbeau's 'Branle de l'Official', harmonised by Wood with all his fastidious professorial craftsmanship.

Woodward's text has all the hallmarks of the received

carol-writer's style. There is the inverted syntax ('in heav'n the bells are ringing'); the archaic vocabulary ('e'en so', 'verily', 'riv'n' – Woodward originally wrote 'the sky is *rent* with angels' singing', which was perhaps a bit obscure, and possibly a bit violent, even for his choristers and congregations); verb forms borrowed from Old English ('sungen' and 'swungen'). Above all there is the fondness for dropping in a Latin refrain, in direct imitation of the macaronic carols of the fifteenth century: '*Gloria, Hosanna in excelsis.*' This creates a seemingly endless melisma (where a single syllable is sung to an extended musical phrase). Other carols with roots in French popular song have this feature too, and it gives them a very distinctive character. It works. No doubt the harmonious marriage of tune and words derives much of its appeal from the influence of one of Woodward's hobbies, bellringing (if not from his other, beekeeping).

The words are, in truth, a bit odd. It's one of the curiosities of this history that some of the wilder flights of Victorian versifying have had much scorn heaped down on their heads, while others, including this one, have apparently passed the test of public acceptability without comment. It doesn't always seem logical. But, of course, liking something doesn't need logic. Woodward's words swing along very happily, the syllables matched gratefully to the chattering rhythm of the verses between the fluid *legato* refrain. It's short, and a welcome chance for the choir to sing something fast. Perhaps all this matters just as much as the words actually meaning anything.

One of the interesting things about scraping away at the history of the music is the chance to experience these tunes as they were before they became the carols we know today.

Often, this means singing them to completely different words. In this case, it means getting up out of your chair and dancing the 'branle'. Try it: Arbeau gives us the clearest possible lesson in how to do it, a sort of sixteenth-century exercise video.

> *Pied gaulche largy* means 'put your left foot out'.
> *Petit sault* is a 'little jump'.
> *Pied droit approché* is 'bring your right foot in'.
> *Pieds ioincts* is 'feet together'.
> Then you make a *double a droict* (do the same four steps to the right).
> Then when you're happy with that you can *empoigner la femme par le saulx du corps* (grab the lady round the waist), *l'eslevant en l'air pour la faire saulter* (pick her up as if she's jumping), then ...
> ... and ... *pause*.
> *Très bien.*

It might not go in your carol service, but it should be fun at the party afterwards.

> *Alors, encore une fois: Un, deux, trois ...*

DE THOINOT ARBEAV. 51
Tabulature du branle de l'Official.

Air de ce branle.   Mouuements d'iceluy.

pied gaulche largy.
petit sault.
pied droit approché.
petit sault.
Pied gaulche largy.
petit sault.
Pieds ioincts.
petit sault.
Pied largy droit.
petit sault.
pied gaulche approché.
petit sault.
pied largy droit.
petit sault.
Pieds ioincts.
petit sault.
Pied gaulche largy.
petit sault.
pieds ioincts.

petit sault.
pied largy gaulche.
petit sault.
Pieds ioincts.
petit sault.
pied largy gaulche.
petit sault.

Ces quatre pas font vn double a gaulche.

Ces quatre pas font vn double a droict.

Pendant ces pas icy, les danceurs vont tousiours du cousté gaulche, sans diuertir a droict.

ORCHESOGRAPHIE

Continuation de l'air.   Continuation des mouuements.

pieds ioincts.
petit sault.
pied largy gaulche.
petit sault.
pieds ioincts.
petit sault.
pied largy gaulche.
petit sault.
pieds ioincts.
petit sault.
pied largy gaulche.
petit sault.
pieds ioincts.
Pied en l'air gaulche.
Pied en l'air droit.
pieds ioincts.
pause.

La continuation de ces mouuements icy, se fait tousiours a gaulche, sans diuertir a droict.

Pendant ces quatre pas icy, l'homme empoigne la femme par le fauls du corps. S'esleuant en l'air pour la faire saulter, & pour ce faire se retourne a la main droitte.

·: 127 :·

'Ding dong! Merrily on High'

E'en so here below, below
Let steeple bells be swungen
And *i-o, i-o, i-o*
By priest and people be sungen
Refrain

Pray ye dutifully prime
Your matin chime, ye ringers
May ye beautifully rime
Your evetime song, ye singers
Refrain

13

∴ Angels from the Realms of Glory ∵

he life story of our next carol contains familiar elements with a personal twist: traditional tune from France combined with words by a Scottish Moravian newspaper editor, one-time prisoner and French Revolution enthusiast based in Sheffield.

At least in this case the tune possibly had some association with Christmas to start with. 'Noëls' are tunes, once played by piping shepherd boys on the mountainsides of Provence and the Pyrenees. In the eighteenth century, published collections of Christmas Noëls were issued. Often, these volumes are the earliest source. There is, however, nothing to suggest that they were newly composed at the time of publication, so it is reasonable to infer that they have their origins in folk music, as their style strongly suggests. Many of them have the triple-time rhythm and rustic, dancelike qualities which Baroque composers used as a convenient shorthand for the bucolic (think of *Messiah*, and concertos by Corelli and Vivaldi). French composers liked to base florid little organ pieces on them, and there are many examples by Daquin and others.

Noëls were also sung in church. Sometimes they were incorporated into liturgical settings, with the words of the Mass or other proper text added to them. The best example is the 'Messe de Minuit' by Marc-Antoine Charpentier, where a number of these tunes process cheerfully through the Mass, sometimes as instrumental interludes with the names of the tunes attached ('Joseph est bien marié', 'Ou s'en vont ces gais bergers', 'A minuit fut fait un réveil') at other times as the musical basis for arty little treble solos ('dessus') and learned fugues. The tunes scrub up very prettily, brought in from the fields to add a little rustic charm to Christmas festivities at the Bourbon court and the gilded churches of Parisian society, the musical equivalent of Marie-Antoinette's shampooed sheep down the hill at the Petit Trianon.

Another way of turning these tunes into sacred music was for the eighteenth-century publishers to give them brand-new words. Often these are evocations of suitable biblical scenes: shepherds dancing, babies sleeping, angels singing. Sometimes they take the form of mini-plays with named characters taking part in a narrative dialogue. The words were probably written by priests, and have none of the dark, atavistic mystery of real folk-carols from the Celtic fringes of Europe, with their strange, pagan imagery of ravens and holly, of life and death.

'Les anges dans nos campagnes' doesn't exist in any surviving printed source before the 1840s, but references and stylistic evidence strongly suggest origins in the eighteenth-century Noël repertoire. The words we sing to its melody today also appeared in print in the first half of the nineteenth century.

James Montgomery had one of the more rackety among many dodgy careers in this book. He was born in Ayrshire in 1771, the son of Moravian missionaries who sent him to a boarding school in Leeds while they sailed off to spread the gospel in the West Indies, where both soon died. The

Moravian school in Leeds didn't allow the study of secular subjects, but young James developed an abiding interest in epic poetry. Perhaps unsurprisingly, under the circumstances, his school career was a failure, and he was sent as apprentice to a baker in Yorkshire. He continued to write poetry in the popular romantic manner, and had some success, though an attempt to forge a literary career in London failed, leading him to return north. He became a journalist, for which his literary instincts were singularly unsuited, working on a paper called the *Sheffield Register*. Unusually, the *Register* took a strongly reformist line on libertarian issues such as the abolition of slavery and proper regulation of boxing, and in 1794 its editor, Joseph Gales, fled to Europe after troops arrived to arrest him for his public support of nascent revolutionary movements across the channel. Montgomery became editor in his stead, changing the name to the slightly more poetic *Sheffield Iris*. He maintained the paper's reforming zeal, and was twice imprisoned for libel, once for publishing a poem celebrating the storming of the Bastille (which may actually have been printed by his predecessor, not by him). Throughout, he wrote poetry. His themes exemplify the best and the worst of a particular kind of high-minded, free-thinking, early nineteenth-century dissenting Christianity. His opposition to slavery is resolute:

> Let tyrants scorn, while tyrants dare,
> The shrieks and writhings of despair;
> An end will come – it will not wait,
> Bonds, yokes, and scourges have their date,
> Slavery itself must pass away,
> And be a tale of yesterday.

Then there is a disturbing poem titled 'An Indian Mother about to Destroy her Child', showing her 'brooding o'er her sex's wrongs' before a graphic description of the crime, a white lotus-leaf wrapped round the baby's mouth to 'still its cries'. Another poem has an Englishwoman gazing at a painting of 'an Aged Negro-Woman' and asking:

> Art thou a woman? ...
> Look on thyself, thy kindred, home, and country,
> Then fall upon thy knees, and cry 'Thank GOD,
> An English woman cannot be a SLAVE!'

Montgomery's best poems are his hymns. In 1825, ownership of the paper passed to a rival, and Montgomery devoted the rest of his life to hymn writing. He was very good at it. Of his 400 or so hymns, a full 100 found a regular place in the repertoire. Several have it still. As with all the best devotional lyricists, part of Montgomery's trick is a profound and easy familiarity with the rich heritage of English liturgical writing, particularly the psalms.

In 1817, a new vicar, the Reverend James Cotterill, arrived at Sheffield's main parish church. Some years before Cotterill had published *A Selection of Psalms and Hymns Adapted to the Services of the Church of England*, but found his new parishioners unwilling to use his carefully crafted versions. In an inspired move, he turned for help to his local newspaper editor, James Montgomery. Metrical versions of psalms, specifically aimed at the practical needs of ordinary worshippers, had been the backbone of congregational singing in England since the Reformation, and they were hugely popular. Montgomery was taking his place in a noble tradition. Their key features are a regular metre (allowing them to be sung to any suitable tune which the congregation already knows), striking imagery and directness of language. To a born-and-bred nonconformist like Montgomery, this was mother's milk. His version of Cotterill's collection achieved widespread use. Countless collections, and hundreds of hymns, soon followed.

'Angels from the Realms of Glory' first saw the light of day in the *Iris* on Christmas Eve, 1816. The path by which Montgomery's poem became linked to the tune published three decades later as 'Les anges dans nos campagnes' is, as usual, complex and sometimes obscured by the historical undergrowth.

It is not clear which, if any, tune Montgomery intended for these words. By writing in the aptly named 'common metre' (albeit with a two-line refrain added to each verse), he may have been inviting his readers to sing it to any tune they liked which happened to fit, a time-honoured way of doing things. Whatever his intentions, his text proved highly popular in song books and ballad sheets.

Meanwhile, the appearance of the Noël 'Les anges dans nos campagnes' in print appears to have led to a number of English translations and paraphrases. One such, 'The Angels we have Heard on High', by the Roman Catholic Bishop of Newcastle, appeared in 1860, set to a simplified version of the original French tune. This version then took on something of a life of its own, for some reason becoming part of the traditional carol repertory in the West Country.

The story now heads south to London and another in our cast of colourful Victorian characters, Henry Smart. Smart was one of the finest organists of his day, a genius in the art of congregational accompaniment, and almost totally blind. In 1867, he edited (largely by dictation to his daughter Ellen) the *Psalms and Hymns for Divine Worship*. Among the tunes is his own 'Regent Square' (named after a posh bit of Regency Bloomsbury) which, it turns out, fits Montgomery's poem splendidly. The story could happily have ended here. However, in 1928, the editors of the *Oxford Book of Carols*, presumably having noticed the similarity between the opening of Montgomery's poem and the old French Noël, decided this was reason enough to graft his words on to its original tune. It doesn't fit terribly well. Why would it? The old tune was intended for words in a different language (if, indeed, it was intended for words at all).

Whatever the complex history of continental cross-pollination which led to this point, there are now several hybrids of the original tune lined up in the musical greenhouse. From here they begin to shoot off in all directions. Far from uniquely in these stories of carols, different branches of the family tree prospered on opposite sides of the Atlantic. American choirs and congregations use Smart's 'Regent Square' for the words. English churches prefer the old French tune which, by a pleasingly illogical association of ideas, has become known as 'Iris'. (The English, incidentally, sing 'Regent Square' to other words, including the mangled Victorian verbiage beginning 'Light's Abode, Celestial Salem'.)

And that's not the end of the matter. Far from it. For some reason the editors of the 1928 Oxford book chose not to use the simple but stirring two-line refrain with which Montgomery ends each verse. Instead they appropriated the equivalent refrain from the original Noël, which isn't in either English or French but in a third language, Latin.

Neither line really works. The Latin has a different number of syllables and the lines have to be shoe-horned rather awkwardly onto the extended melisma at this point in the tune. Smart's rising sequence makes much better sense of the repetition of 'Come and worship'. The editors had not quite got over the persistent enthusiasm for the macaronic refrain. The irony is that nothing could be less appropriate in a poem by an early nineteenth-century Scots Dissenter. Montgomery would have been appalled.

Thus we find ourselves with three basic incarnations of this carol (with countless variants among and between them). In the US, Smart's tune 'Regent Square' is sung with Montgomery's words (English refrain). In the UK, the French folk tune known as 'Iris' is sung with Montgomery's words (Latin refrain, usually; English refrain, sometimes). The 'simplified' version of the French tune also prospers, most commonly to the words beginning 'Angels we have heard on high', with many other variants including 'Shepherds in the fields abiding' (which, to confuse matters further, is the first line of Montgomery's second verse, but continues quite differently).

It's the sort of intriguing muddle with which readers of this book will now be familiar. And somewhere underneath it all is the curious idea that today we find ourselves singing a tune which may, just possibly, have been one of the musical candle-flames around which the gilded moths flitted and flickered at the court of Louis XIV, to words by a man who spent a good part of his career articulating the ideas which eventually brought that court to its blooded knees. Happy Christmas, Louis.

'Angels from the Realms of Glory'

Shepherds, in the fields abiding,
Watching o'er your flocks by night,
God with man is now residing,
Yonder shines the infant light:
Refrain

Sages, leave your contemplations,
Brighter visions beam afar;
Seek the great Desire of nations,
Ye have seen his natal star:
Refrain

Sinners, wrung with true repentance,
Doomed for guilt to endless pains,
Justice now revokes the sentence,
Mercy calls you – break your chains:
Refrain

Though an infant now we view him,
He shall fill his Father's throne,
Gather all the nations to him;
Every knee shall then bow down:
Refrain

All creation, join in praising
God the Father, Spirit, Son,
Evermore your voices raising,
To th'eternal Three in One:
Refrain

·: Hark, the Herald Angels Sing :·

f we think about it at all, we probably think this hymn was written by Charles Wesley (words) and Felix Mendelssohn (music). The tune is called 'Mendelssohn', after all.

Well, up to a point. Although they were certainly the prime movers, so many others have had a hand in fashioning the carol as we know it today that Wesley and Mendelssohn may be regarded as not so much even 'primi inter pares' ('first among equals') as 'pares inter pares' ('equals among equals').

The words first. This poem is by Charles Wesley the elder, father of Methodism and of a talented, successful and badly behaved family. Isn't it?

In fact, we get through precisely one word of Wesley's poem before we find ourselves singing alterations and inter-polations added by other hands. The forensically complex process by which this hymn has mutated from Wesley's original tells us something important about Methodism and its leading early practitioners.

Hymns were their life-blood. This was an itinerant church, pioneering the concept of large-scale meetings, often held outdoors, and making long journeys on foot to spread the gospel. Stirring, striding hymns are an essential ingredient of both kinds of informal, *al fresco* worship. Charles

Wesley alone is thought to have written over 6,000, typically with ten or twenty verses each. Methodist hymn books and collections of verse often went through multiple editions to keep up with demand, and, just like the much-reprinted psalters of the sixteenth and seventeenth centuries, the texts evolved as they went along, no doubt partly in response to what people actually sang.

At the same time, this was a church which militated strongly against central authority. If a particular preacher or hymn leader wanted to emphasise or develop a particular point of doctrine, that was between him, God and his congregation. These men could, on occasion, disagree deeply about such things. So if one of them chose to alter an existing hymn to his own purposes, nobody, least of all the original author, had the right to tell him not to. There was no copyright to be jealously guarded, and in any event, notions of individual authorship were less strongly developed: in very many cases authorship is not ascribed at all, leaving it unclear whether a hymn is by Charles or John, or both, or someone else entirely. It was, at least up to a point, understood and accepted that this is a collaborative process.

This carol, then, bears the imprint of some strong and colourful personalities.

To begin with, here is the text as Charles Wesley first published it in the 1739 edition of *Hymns and Sacred Poems*:

> Hark how all the welkin rings
> 'Glory to the King of kings,
> Peace on earth, and mercy mild,
> God and sinners reconcil'd!'

Joyful all ye nations rise,
Join the triumph of the skies,
Universal nature say
'Christ the Lord is born to day!'

Christ, by highest heav'n ador'd,
Christ, the everlasting Lord,
Late in time behold him come,
Offspring of a virgin's womb.

Veil'd in flesh, the Godhead see,
Hail th' incarnate deity!
Pleas'd as man with men t' appear
Jesus, our Immanuel here!

Hail the heav'nly Prince of Peace!
Hail the Sun of righteousness!
Light and life to all he brings,
Ris'n with healing in his wings.

Mild he lays his glory by,
Born – that man no more may die,
Born – to raise the sons of earth,
Born – to give them second birth.

Come, desire of nations, come,
Fix in us thy humble home,
Rise, the woman's conqu'ring seed,
Bruise in us the serpent's head.

Starting as early as the second edition later that same year, and on through the many subsequent re-printings, small changes creep in. It was subjected to more substantial editorial attention in a 1758 volume edited by George Whitefield.

Whitefield had been a member of the Wesley brothers' 'Holy Club' at Christ Church, Oxford (mockingly christened 'methodists' by their fellow undergraduates for their prim, methodical ways). He was a passionate preacher, pioneer of the mass-meeting and an intrepid traveller. His journeys took him to Bermuda, Ireland and Gibraltar. He visited America seven times, becoming a real celebrity there. Benjamin Franklin invited him to stay in his house, and remembered that 'He replied, that if I made that kind Offer for Christ's sake, I should not miss of a Reward. And I return'd, Don't let me be mistaken; it was not for Christ's sake, but for your sake'. Franklin also conducted a typically scientific experiment to work out how many people could comfortably hear Whitefield's 'loud and clear voice' when he was preaching outside. He made it 30,000.

Back in England, Whitefield had a go at Wesley's opening couplet, turning

Hark, how all the welkin rings!
Glory to the King of kings.

into

Hark, the herald-angels sing,
Glory to the new-born King!

Further changes followed in 1760 at the hand of Martin Madan, priest, lawyer, Calvinist, yet another former Christ Church man and author of an embarrassingly enthusiastic treatise on polygamy.

Apart from altering some of the words, the main change in these later versions is the reduction in the number of verses, partly, perhaps, to skirt gently around some of the knottier theology about original sin and whose fault it was. By the time Sandys included 'Hark, the Herald' in his collections of 1833 and 1852, there are five verses, with the opening couplet of verse one used as a refrain, just as we do today. The text has reached its modern form (except that the verses still have four lines each, as in Wesley, rather than the later eight).

Do the changes improve Wesley's hymn? Some think so. Some commentators believe that Wesley wrote so much and so quickly that he allowed bad poetry to stand alongside good, sometimes in the same work (perhaps unsurprising when your known output of hymns and other poems totals over 9,000). Many of his texts were edited by others for publication. He expected it. And Whitefield was only tidying up uncomfortable archaisms like 'welkin'.

But, on the other hand, 'welkin' is a perfectly respect-able English word. Shakespeare uses it. It means the sky, the firmament, the heavens. It is, in fact, the right word for the scene of the angels' airborne performance that night. Also, the word-stress of the phrase 'Hark, the herald-angels' puts the accent too much on the herald part, not the angels: 'hark, the angel-heralds' would have been better. And (without getting too deep into Biblical exegesis) 'King of kings' is certainly more inspiring than 'new-born king'. It's a quote from the Book of Revelation (and Handel's very-nearly contemporary 'Messiah'). It separates out this king from all others, which 'new-born king' does not. And there is something gloriously inclusive, almost pantheistic, something of the spirit of Addison, in Wesley's lines:

Universal nature say
'Christ the Lord is born today!'

Much better than Whitefield's replacement:

> With th'Angelic hosts proclaim,
> Christ is born in Bethlehem!

which doesn't rhyme and puts a whopping accent on the last syllable of 'Bethlehem' (which he also does later to the word 'Emmanuel' by making it a four rather than a three-syllable word).

The Wesleys didn't like people changing their hymns. John said:

> Many gentlemen have done my brother and me (though without naming us) the honour to reprint many of our Hymns. Now they are perfectly welcome so to do, provided they print them just as they are. But I desire they would not attempt to mend them; for they really are not able. None of them is able to mend either the sense or the verse.
>
> Therefore, I must beg of them one of these two favours; either to let them stand just as they are, to take them for better for worse; or to add the true reading in the margin, or at the bottom of the page; that we may no longer be accountable either for the nonsense or for the doggerel of other men.

Well, quite.

Unfortunately for Wesley senior, it doesn't matter what he begs. People sing it like this because they like it like this, and they like it because they know it. Some twentieth-century editors, including Vaughan Williams, tried to restore Wesley's welkins: congregations just laughed. Usage is sanctified by habit. Hamlet was right: 'there is nothing either good or bad but thinking makes it so'. Or, perhaps, not thinking.

By using four-line stanzas in a regular metre, Charles Wesley created a hymn which could be sung to a number of tunes. Candidates include 'Savannah' (sung today to 'Love's Redeeming Work is Done') which John Wesley had recently imported from the Moravians, and 'Easter Hymn' from the *Lyra Davidica* book of 1708 ('Jesus Christ is Risen Today'), complete with Alleluias, a splendidly rousing and Christ-massy way to do it. Later (but pre-'Mendelssohn') hymnals use 'Salzburg' ('At the Lamb's High Feast We Sing' or 'Songs of Thankfulness and Praise'), which is an eight-line tune.

The Mendelssohn connection came later. You can find it stated that Mendelssohn didn't like it. This is a misreading. He didn't like some other words which an English poet put to this music, and said so. But he didn't know about the Wesley connection, which was made six years after his death. And the man who made it didn't know about Mendelssohn's objection to the earlier effort.

In 1840, Mendelssohn fulfilled a commission for a cantata to mark the 400th anniversary of Gutenberg's invention of movable type. Overleaf is movement two, with its solidly Germanic scoring for men's voices and brass band.

Mendelssohn's English publisher, Ewer and Co., had it translated into English by a Mr Bartholomew. Mendelssohn wasn't impressed:

> I must repeat the wish I already expressed in my letter to Mr. Bartholomew. I think there ought to be other words to No. 2, the 'Lied'. If the right ones are hit at, I am sure that piece will be liked very much by the singers and the hearers, but it will never do to sacred words. There must be a national and merry subject found out, something to which the soldierlike and buxom motion of the piece has

Hark, the Herald Angels Sing

some relation, and the words must express something gay
and popular, as the music tries to do it.

Mendelssohn is writing in his second language here, but
choirs could still do well to try and follow his instruction
to be more 'soldierlike and buxom' next time they sing this
tune.

In England, Mendelssohn was a superstar. He visited
many times. One of his favourite musical haunts was St
Paul's Cathedral, where his old friend Thomas Attwood
('dear old Attwood') was organist. On one of his last visits,
in 1847, Mendelssohn conducted the London premiere of
his oratorio *Elijah*. Among the choristers was a sixteen-year-
old St Paul's Cathedral choirboy called William Hayman
Cummings.

Cummings was born in Sidbury, Devon, in 1831. He sang
as a boy at both St Paul's and the Temple Church, and in
adulthood was an accomplished tenor (once taking the solo
in a new cantata by Arthur Sullivan, apparently at just thirty
minutes' notice), professor of singing at the Royal Academy
of Music, principal of the Guildhall School and a Gentleman
of the Chapel Royal. In the early part of his professional
career he was organist of Waltham Abbey in Essex (Tallis's
old church). The *Musical Times* takes up the story some
decades later, in 1897:

> Mr. Cummings informs us that he eagerly procured every-
> thing that Mendelssohn composed as soon as it was
> published. While playing over the chorus in G he was at
> once struck by its adaptability to the words 'Hark! the
> herald angels sing'. He copied out the parts, and the tune
> was sung with great enthusiasm by the congregation at

Waltham Abbey. He soon afterwards began to receive so many applications for manuscript copies that he took his arrangement to Messrs. Ewer and Co., who published it in 1856.

'Hark (etc…)' in Charles Wesley's own handwriting.

A nice irony that this is the same publishing house firmly told by Mendelssohn that the tune would 'never do to sacred words'.

The 'great enthusiasm' Cummings found for his marriage of Mendelssohn and Wesley led to its inclusion in *Hymns Ancient and Modern* in 1861.

There are, of course, a number of changes between Mendelssohn's chorus and Cummings's hymn. The third verse, in the minor, has gone. The tune is extrapolated rather ingeniously from the original by following it from vocal to instrumental parts and back again in the third phrase. Cummings has smoothed out a number of dotted rhythms. Had he lived to do so, Mendelssohn might well have believed himself justified in echoing Wesley's wail of a hundred years before.

But at least one of the changes was neither Cummings's fault nor to his liking, as the *Musical Times* makes clear: ' ... as Mr. Cummings justly says, an unwarrantable alteration has been made in the melody by the introduction of a B at the third beat of bar twelve which Mendelssohn did not write.' Cummings, mender of Mendelssohn, has been mended in his turn.

Mended or mangled, this one stuck. Words and music have passed through many hands, some unknown, to reach the familiar form we know today. They have appeared in pretty much every carol book since 1861. Mendelssohn's soldierlike and buxom paean to movable type has helped perpetuate the legacy of Johannes Gutenberg in a way he could never have foreseen.

'Hark, the Herald Angels Sing'

Christ, by highest heaven adored,
Christ, the everlasting lord
Late in time behold Him come,
Off-spring of a Virgin's womb
Veiled in flesh the Godhead see,
Hail, the incarnate deity
Pleased as Man with men to dwell,
Jesus, our Emmanuel.
Hark! the herald angels sing,
'Glory to the New-born king!'

Hail the heav'n-born Prince of Peace,
Hail, the Sun of Righteousness
Light and life to all He brings,
Risen with healing in His Wings.
Now He lays His Glory by,
Born that man no more may die
Born to raise the sons of earth,
Born to give them second birth.
Hark! the herald angels sing,
'Glory to the New-born king!'

15

·: The Christ-child's Lullaby :·

eltic Christianity had character. Its rugged outposts in Brittany and Cornwall, St David's on its rocky Welsh promontory and the monastery island of Skellig Michael sticking out of the Atlantic off the west coast of Ireland, speak to us of some of the earliest and toughest Christians we have. Led by Brigid and Patrick, Petroc and Ninian, they let the wind and waves decide where they would settle and pray along the ragged fringes of the known world, rough places 'nourished by salt winds', as the Welsh poet and priest R. S. Thomas says of an Irish shrine, the Celtic corners of Europe, sharing an inheritance of carvings and crosses, place-names and burial mounds, saints, seabirds and rain.

Celtic culture laid down a rich artistic seam. Seekers and dreamers have found much to explore. Manuscripts such as the *Book of Kells* tell of an age of accomplishment and piety. The Celtic cross remains one of our most potent symbols. Their music, as in all churches, served different functions and drew on different sources. Liturgical music was chant, the Roman kind brought over by Augustine, the sort of singing a journeying monk would have recognised, more or less, at any abbey or large church in western Europe in the second half of the first millennium and beyond. Differences, where they exist, are in details of liturgical practice and, no doubt, a local accent to words and music.

Then there are sacred and devotional folk songs, to sing while clinging to your wicker and leather coracle as you paddle perilously across to Skellig Michael or up to Iona, the music of sky and tide. Eternity, and Ninian's God, are close.

And there are carols. The Breton Carol, the Wexford Carol, the St Ives Carol 'Hellesveor', bard songs of Wales: these are our lullaby's cousins across the water.

Columba took Christianity north in the sixth century. The centre of his new settlement was Iona, in the Hebrides, the nearest point to his native Ireland. From there, Christianity with a Celtic tinge spread through Scotland and across to the north-east of England and the familiar remoteness of Lindisfarne. Religion around these coasts has always received much of its influence from across the sea. Churches, and what happens inside them, echo with the voice of the Viking as much as the Irish saint. John Knox brought his stern brand of Puritanism back from Geneva to the metropolitan areas of Scotland. But in the remoter wilds of the north and west, Catholicism had roots strong enough to withstand any vain blasts of the doctrinal trumpet.

All this is present in the folk music of the Highlands and Islands, distilled into something potent and unique. This carol touches a different aspect of our tradition from the others in the book. It has found a home not so much in the choir stall and among troupes of carollers as in the repertoire of traditional folk singers and bands.

Father Ronald (or Ranald) Rankin was Roman Catholic parish priest of Moidart, a remote colony of townships clustered on the shores of Loch Shiel to the west of Fort William, just over the sea from Skye, from 1834–55, a hundred short years after these hillsides had cheered Bonnie Prince Charlie off on his doomed march south. In his churchmanship and approach to music Rankin combined the dictates of Rome with local customs and habits, just as Columba had done. Celtic folk music, and the folk song of the highlands and islands in particular, has a number of types which are quite distinct from the native traditions of the rest of the British Isles.

'Waulking' is beating newly woven tweed to soften it and stop it shrinking in the ever-present rain. It was done by large groups of women sitting either side of a long board or table, and like many such repetitive, labour-intensive manual tasks, it had a highly developed repertoire of songs to go with it. The nature of the task dictates the nature of the song. A leader sings the verses, the chorus of women either repeating what they've heard, like the 'lining-out' in Gaelic psalms, or singing an alternating refrain. The rhythm of the music matches the rhythm of the work. There are many verses.

Rankin borrowed aspects of this tradition when he wrote his Gaelic poem 'Taladh Ar Slanuighear', 'The Lullaby of the Saviour'. He used the multiple verse structure learnt from his parishioners. He borrowed one of their melodies. One archive copy of the song tells us that he inscribed the song 'Cuimhneachan do Chloinn Mhuideart bho Raonall Mac-Raing': 'a memento for the children of Moidart of (or 'by') Raonall Mac-Raing', a touching insight into the musical side of his ministry, especially since 'these copies were circulated among the Parishioners on the emigration of the Author to Australia'.

The tune Fr Rankin intended for his poem was the 'Air

Fonn "Cumha Mhic Arois"', the 'tune of "Grief for the Son of Arois"', a characteristically violent and long-winded lament for a high-spirited young man who was drowned by an unruly horse (which, like many of the old Scots ballads, may actually be true). Typically, however, the tune (or tunes) to which it is now sung are variants or countermelodies to the ballad tune, not the tune itself. There are several, related melodies.

For one, we turn with admiration and gratitude to the substantial achievement of one of our most dedicated and single-minded folklorists. Marjory Kennedy-Fraser came from a musical family. Her father was a well-known singer of traditional song, and several of her siblings became professional musicians. Widowed at the age of thirty-three, she supported herself by working as a music teacher and lecturer in Edinburgh, developing at the same time a passionate interest in Celtic culture. With a fellow-enthusiast, the painter John Duncan, she made many visits to Eriskay and the Western Isles, and from 1909 published four volumes of *Songs of the Hebrides* in her own arrangements for voice and piano, with texts in Gaelic and English. All island life is here: spinning songs and longing songs, 'The Crone's Creel' and 'The Loch Broom Love Song'; and, always, there is the sea, rising and falling in the sad, keening refrains of love and loss.

There are two seasonal sacred songs: 'Christmas Duanag' and 'Taladh Chriosda', which is Rankin's cradle-song under a slightly different name: 'The Christ-Child's Lullaby'.

Kennedy-Fraser heard the 'Lullaby' sung by Mrs John MacInnes of Eriskay. The tune is a thing of melting grace, haunting yet calm, enough almost to still the raging of the sea. She subsequently found Rankin's complete text (twenty-nine verses) in a hymn book compiled by one of his successors, the 'King-Priest of Eriskay', Fr Allan MacDonald.

In another version of the tune the notes are identical except that the third degree of the scale is lowered instead of raised (or, in folk parlance, 'weakened' rather than 'strengthened'), taking the song from a 'major' sounding mode to a 'minor', a striking change.

A third version has a different first line but is the same after that. This is the one sung by many modern folk singers and bands. Simplicity lends itself to all sorts of approaches. It keeps up its attendance in church, too, once a year, at Midnight Mass in the Outer Hebrides, in the dark part of the year. It is a song rooted in its native rocky soil. Like so many other authors and musicians, Father Rankin was as much contributing to an existing tradition as writing something new. The song has other links to the folk traditions of the Isles, too, in particular a story about how it first came to be heard there.

'In Eigg and Uist this lullaby was associated with a legend', says Kennedy-Fraser:

> There was once a shiftless laddie in one of the isles who had lost his mother, and that is always a sad tale, but had got a stepmother in her place, and that is sometimes a sadder tale still ... 'Son of another,' said his stepmother in the heat of anger, 'there will be no luck in this house till you leave; but whoever heard of a luckless chick leaving of its own will?' But leave the shiftless laddie did, and that of his own will, and ere the full moon rose at night, he was on the other side of the ben.

From the 'Book of Kells': the earliest representation of Virgin and child in a Western manuscript. The accompanying text begins 'Nativitatem Christi in Bethlehem'

That night the stepmother could get neither sleep nor ease; there was something ringing in her ear, and something else stinging in her heart, until at last her bed was like a cairn of stones in a forest of reptiles. 'I will rise', she said, 'and see if the night outside is better than the night inside.' She rose and went out, with her face towards the ben; nor did she ever stop until she saw something which made her stop. What was this but a Woman, with the very heat-love of Heaven in her face, sitting on a grassy knoll and song-lulling a baby-son with the sweetest music ever heard under moon or sun; and at her feet was the shiftless laddie, his face like the dream of the Lord's night. 'God of the Graces!' said the stepmother. 'It is Mary-Mother, and she is doing what I ought to be doing – song-lulling the orphan.' And she fell on her knees and began to weep the soft, warm tears of a mother: and when, after a while, she looked up, there was nobody there but herself and the shiftless laddie side by side.

And that is how the Christ's lullaby was heard in the isles.

'The Christ-child's Lullaby'

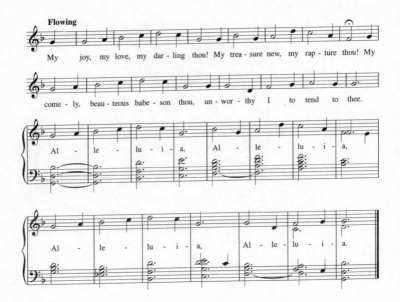

Flowing

My joy, my love, my dar - ling thou! My trea - sure new, my rap - ture thou! My

come - ly, beau - teous babe - son thou, un - wor - thy I to tend to thee.

Al - le - lu - i - a, Al - le - lu - i - a,

Al - le - lu - i - a, Al - le - lu - i - a.

While sun of hope and light art thou!
Of love the heart and eye art thou!
Though but a tender babe, I bow
In heavenly rapture unto thee.

And though thou art the King of all
They sent thee to the manger-stall
Where at thy feet they all shall fall
And sing their praises unto thee.

16

·: Away in a Manger :·

n a 1996 poll to find the most popular Christmas carols in the UK, 'Away in a Manger' came second. Not bad for a youngster.

This one's only been around for about 130 years. In that time it has garnered more tunes than probably any other carol. It has also generated considerable confusion about who wrote it, a misattribution to Luther, and a minor theological controversy.

In 1884 this appeared in a Boston publication called *The Myrtle*:

Luther 's Cradle Song.

Martin Luther, the great German reformer, who was born four hundred years ago the 10th of next November, composed the following hymn for his children ; and it is still sung by many German mothers to their little ones : —

Away in a manger,
No crib for his bed,
The little Lord Jesus
Lay down his sweet head.
The stars in the sky
Looked down where he lay,
The little Lord Jesus
Asleep in the hay.

The cattle are lowing,
The poor baby wakes ;
But little Lord Jesus,
No crying he makes,
I love thee, Lord Jesus :
Look down from the sky,
And stay by my crib,
Watching my lullaby.

It may be sung to the air of "Home, Sweet Home."

It's an intriguing item. For one thing, the paper states as a fact that the text is by Martin Luther. It isn't. Luther wrote lots of hymns, but he didn't write this one. Deliberately or otherwise, the editors have confidently misinformed their readers, for reasons which may or may not be connected with a series of pageants and celebrations which were held in Boston and the surrounding area to mark the four-hundredth anniversary of Luther's birth (which was actually a year earlier, anyway). It stuck. The hymn appeared in print many times with his name attached in the following decades, often under the unambiguous title 'Luther's Cradle Hymn'. Lots of children have been lulled to sleep by these words. Luther's own *neugeboren kinder* were not among them.

Another interesting feature is that the words, not untypically for a Christmas carol, are not quite as we know them today. Change has not necessarily meant improvement. The image of the Christ-child 'watching my lullaby' is a touching one, perhaps better than the faux-archaic 'stay by my bedside 'til morning is nigh' which has replaced it. The poem is also one syllable short in a few places, for example in line five, necessitating the later addition of the metrically regular but meteorologically questionable adjective 'bright' for the night sky.

As well as no author, there is no tune. It's a fascinating thought that the editors expected their lyric to be sung to Henry Bishop's parlour song 'Home! Sweet Home!' This tune, with words by the American John Howard Payne and based (according to Bishop) on a Sicilian folk song, was vastly popular in the US. Both sides in the Civil War adopted it. Lincoln had it sung at the White House. Its message of the heartfelt peace and sanctity of the family home make it the perfect fit for this quiet little household prayer over the sleeping child. Try it. See?

Despite, or perhaps because of, this lack of an authorised melody, composers treated the text as fair game for their own inventions, inspired no doubt by the simple charm of the imagery and the gentle, rocking triple-time metre (an unusual feature: there are some traditional carol tunes with three beats to the bar or half-bar, but they tend to work by elongating the first syllable of groups of two, for example 'In dulci jubilo' and 'Quem pastores'). The vast majority of the specially composed tunes to 'Away in a Manger' are, unlike 'Home! Sweet Home!' in some version of three-time.

Then, in 1892, a third verse appeared. This, too, has been misattributed. It may well be by Charles H. Gabriel, who edited the book in which it was first printed and wrote the tune which lives with it there. Bishop William Anderson later claimed that the third verse was written at his request by Dr John T. MacFarland, the secretary of his Board of Sunday Schools, for Children's Day. Again, the attribution persisted, and again, it is erroneous. Anderson's publication post-dated Gabriel's by more than a decade. In fact, like so many of its older brethren, it's impossible to say for certain who wrote the words.

The theological controversy centres on the line 'the little Lord Jesus, no crying he makes', which has been taken by some as denying Christ the full attributes of humanity by not behaving like a real human child, a heresy known as 'Docetism'. This is certainly not the place to become entwined in doctrinal niceties, except perhaps to observe that this is far from the only occasion in our carol repertoire where a poet is filling in with a bit of local colour of his own.

The Gospels tell us almost nothing about Christ's infancy and early life, and many of its most familiar features are later inventions and embellishments, hallowed by long use: the animals peering patiently at us from inside the stable, source of inspiration alike to the greatest masters of Renaissance art and the costume ladies of the school Nativity play; the three kings with their crowns and gowns; and, above all, the bleak midwinter. There are no frosty winds in Luke. And anyway, the poet doesn't say that the baby Jesus doesn't cry at all, ever: just not at this particular moment. Perhaps he was distracted by the lowing of the cattle. It seems a harmless enough detail.

In 1951, Richard S. Hill published a thorough and splendidly entertaining article called 'Not So Far Away in a Manger', listing all the musical settings he could find. There are forty-one. Clearly there is no scope (and probably less appetite) for a comprehensive review of the whole lot here (and there are plenty more, both before and since Hill's epic feat of collation and indexing). We limit ourselves here to the two tunes sung most often in, respectively, the UK and the US.

The biographies of the two composers are strikingly similar.

William J. Kirkpatrick was an organist, hymn writer and one-time fife major in the Philadelphia Volunteers. He issued some hundred books of devotional pieces, often with his business partner John R. Sweney. In 1895, they published *Around the World with Christmas. A Christmas Exercise*, a kind of Christmas play. 'Away in a Manger' (under the usual title 'Luther's Cradle Hymn') is 'for singing by the Primary School, or selected scholar'. Kirkpatrick's simple piano arrangement evokes the world of the school song and the camp meeting, with its strong, static bass and well-meaning thirds and sixths.

A nice story neatly captures something of the character of Kirkpatrick and his world. He would often attend large Methodist meetings, organising and leading the music. On one occasion he noticed that the soloist he had engaged to lead the hymns was getting into the habit of leaving before the sermon. Concerned for the state of the young man's soul, he began to turn over the words of a new hymn in his mind:

> I've wandered far away from God,
> Now I'm coming home;
> The paths of sin too long I've trod,
> Lord, I'm coming home.
> Coming home, coming home,
> Nevermore to roam;
> Open now Thine arms of love,
> Lord, I'm coming home.

Kirkpatrick handed the young man his new lyric. Moved, the singer found himself approaching the altar and accepting the preacher's call to 'come home'. Kirkpatrick's tune to 'Away in a Manger' has kept the name originally given to the words, 'Cradle Song'.

James Ramsey Murray, composer of our other tune, also served as an army musician in the Civil War period, studied the art of hymn writing with leading practitioners including the great Lowell Mason, worked in publishing and as a schoolteacher, and wrote a great many hymns. The residual German associations of this one, surface in his version. His tune bears the name 'Mueller', after a certain Carl Mueller, who is credited as the composer in a number of publications but appears in fact to be not just the subject of yet another case of misattribution but entirely fictional. Some have noted a similarity (actually pretty slight), between the opening phrase of Murray's tune and part of a waltz by Johann Strauss the younger (number four of 'Tales from the Vienna Woods'). Perhaps there is a nod here in the direction of the 'Pennsylvania Deutsch' (or 'Dutch'), the large local German population, whose attachment to their compatriot Martin Luther gave birth to this carol in the first place (and caused such confusion thereafter).

Its cradle, *The Myrtle*, was the public voice of the Universalist movement, which seeks a humanity and religion common to all. The other items on the same page convey something of the essence and flavour of the approach. An improving domestic tale ends with the tag-line 'Somebody stands in Christ's place in every home. Who is it in your house?' A butterfly reminds a humming bird (who he first met when he was a caterpillar) to judge not, lest ye be judged: 'Never insult the humble, as they may some day become your superiors'. Some singers have found something similarly sentimental and didactic in 'Away in a Manger'. But there is, too, something rugged and sincere in its emotional hinterland, rooted in the faith and soul of the eastern seaboard of post-Civil War America.

In its short career, this little carol has gone through many of the life experiences of many of its older and wiser brethren. It has lost track of some of its parents, has picked up several more and less suitable partners, and spawned a number of offspring and variants. Like folk song, many of its tunes sound like variations of each other, perhaps because the placing of cadence and metre is almost a natural phenomenon, like similarities of word formation across different languages. Some of the tunes actually fit together, again, like some folk songs.

But there's an artfulness, too. The words shift to the first person in the middle of the second verse, so subtly that we barely notice. Uniquely, we speak in the voice of the actual baby itself, gazing up from the crib with big, round unblinking eyes. Sentimental, certainly: but what could better evoke the sense of appealing to the protection of another baby, far away, in a manger?

It's a folk song for our times; the new old. It's a song about home, safety, and a little, tiny child, sleeping peacefully.

Home, sweet home.

'Away in a Manger'

'Cradle Song'

'Mueller'

Away in a manger, no crib for a bed,
The little Lord Jesus laid down his sweet head.
The stars in the bright sky looked down where he lay
The little Lord Jesus asleep on the hay.

The cattle are lowing, the baby awakes,
But little Lord Jesus no crying he makes.
I love thee, Lord Jesus! look down from the sky.
And stay by my bedside till morning is nigh.

Be near me, Lord Jesus, I ask thee to stay
Close by me for ever, and love me, I pray.
Bless all the dear children in thy tender care,
And take us to heaven to live with thee there.

17

∴ Good King Wenceslas ∴

ew carols have had so much scorn heaped on them as this poor little thing. Elizabeth Poston called it the 'product of an unnatural marriage between Victorian whimsy and the thirteenth-century', which is both 'bizarre' and 'ridiculous'. Several writers have used the word 'doggerel'. One went as far as calling it 'ponderous moral doggerel'. The great Percy Dearmer expressed the pious hope that, 'with the present wealth of carols for Christmas, "Good King Wenceslas" may gradually pass into disuse'.

But it didn't. The fact that Dearmer and Poston were wrong tells us something important about our carol tradition.

Good King Wenceslas wasn't a king, and he wasn't called Wenceslas. But he was good, so our mythologising lyricist scores one out of three for historical accuracy, which is probably better than some. Our hero's real name, in his native Czech, was Vaclav ('Wenceslas' seems to be a German version of the name), and he ruled as duke (not king) of Bohemia in the early tenth century. His family life was a trifle irregular. He was brought up by his grandmother until she was murdered by his mother, who then ruled as regent, but with such cruelty that she in turn was overthrown and exiled by Vaclav. He proved a wise and sympathetic monarch, deeply pious and dedicated to his beloved Catholic church, building many churches and shrines including St Vitus's Cathedral, still standing within the walls of Prague castle. In 935 he was invited to dinner by his own brother, Boleslav, and was murdered. In a plot-twist worthy of 'Macbeth', Boleslav's son was born on the very day of the murder.

There are lots of stories of Vaclav's piety and good works. The tale of the page, the peasant and the pine-logs, of course, isn't one of them. It's fiction: one of those myths that gather around the image of a favourite saint or celebrity.

Almost a thousand years later a Victorian hymn writer and clergyman was looking for material for a new collection of carols. John Mason Neale was a prolific and popular writer. He has a whopping thirty-nine entries in the *New English Hymnal*, more than any other author, thirteen ahead of his nearest rival, Charles Wesley. Among his familiar efforts are 'Jerusalem the Golden', 'All Glory, Laud and Honour', 'Christ is Made the Sure Foundation', 'Come, Ye Faithful, Raise the Anthem', 'The Day of Resurrection', and many others. On this occasion he wanted a carol not for Christmas Day itself but for St Stephen's Day, 26 December, one of the several feast days that fall during the liturgical 'octave', the eight days following a major festival of the church year.

The story of Stephen does not really lend itself to Christmas jollity, so Neale turned instead to the legend of Vaclav, which happens to be set on the right date. The link with Christmas is already looking a bit thin. True, St Stephen's Day is chronologically, if not liturgically, closer to Christmas than some of the events we bundle up together and sing about at Christmas (Advent, Epiphany, the Annunciation). But the Feast of Stephen has nothing to do with Christmas, and anyway the carol is not about Stephen, it's about Wenceslas, whose own feast day is in September. Any remaining tenuous link with the meaning of Christmas has been stretched almost beyond breaking-point.

This was one of the reasons why the brainy chaps of English music and letters took such a dislike to Neale's carol. The other was his verse. Perhaps, at some level, they were nervous about his dangerously subversive message of social equality and redistribution of wealth. This was, after all, the age which readily got to its feet in church to heartily applaud the Almighty's good sense in putting 'the rich man in his castle, the poor man at his gate, God made them high and lowly, and ordered their estate'. Some found his moral tone hectoring and kitsch. Others just thought it was bad poetry. Some tried to untie his more tortured syntax. 'Good my page' becomes, in some later editions, the rather more sensible 'my good page'. But it didn't stick. People didn't like it.

Why? Because, whether we like it or not, a certain kind of sentimental, Victorian cod-mediaevalism rings the right bells. Or, as Neale might have put it, the right bells rings.

But on a more serious level, there is something challenging in Neale's choice of subject-matter for his carol. Wenceslas is a saint of the Catholic church. The story Neale uses is not based on any documented incident in his life. It's a myth. There are pictures of modern-day cardinals, red-hatted and resplendent, carrying Wenceslas's 1,000-year-old skull on a gilded cushion in procession to the altar. This is the sort of thing which the men who founded Neale's church in the sixteenth century absolutely loathed. Is there something slightly disturbing in the idea of an English cleric putting this sort of idolatry into the mouths of English choristers? His contemporaries thought so. Many were deeply distrustful of his brand of high-church Anglo-Catholicism. Once he was attacked at a nun's funeral. Crowds threatened to stone him and burn down his house. His own bishop banned him from ministry for nineteen years.

For his tune, Neale turned to a book published in Finland in 1582. *Piae Cantiones ecclesiasticae velerum episcoporum* is a collection of school songs assembled by Jaako Suomalainen, headmaster of Turku cathedral school. In 1853 a British diplomat brought a copy home to London and gave it to Neale, who in turn shared it with his friend and fellow high-churchman Thomas Helmore, and forth they went together through the task of translating the texts, transcribing the musical notation and turning the results into suitably Victorianised choral arrangements, like some half-forged antique or bad bit of Gilbert Scott.

Few collaborations have produced such a concentration of repertoire items. Among their Christmas hymns are 'O Come, O Come, Emmanuel', 'Of the Father's Love Begotten', 'A Great and Mighty Wonder', 'Good Christian Men, Rejoice' ('In dulci jubilo'), 'Unto Us is Born a Son' ('Puer nobis nascitur'), 'Gabriel's Message Does Away' ('Angelus emittitur'), 'Christ was Born on Christmas Day' ('Resonet in laudibus'), 'Let the Song be Begun' ('Personent hodie'), and many others. Within the manner of their age, Neale and Helmore were scholars, and brought much of the writing and music of the early and eastern churches back into the light of day. They virtually invented the modern use of plainsong.

Jaako Suomalainen, the singing headmaster in the sixteenth-century snows of Finland, used his song book as a vehicle for moral as well as musical instruction. This

was a deeply Protestant notion, a flame still burning reso-
lutely in the England of three centuries later. In 1854, Neale
issued his carols in a 'condensed' version for children, and
several other books aimed at young people. Others did the
same. The carol we know as 'Infant Holy, Infant Lowly', for
example, was imported from its native Poland by Edith M.
Reed and published in *Primary Education: A monthly journal for
Primary Teachers*, vol XXVIII, no. 10, December 1920. Same
idea: turn an exotic original into a polite English carol with a
neat moral and a nice tune, though no doubt Neale's Finnish
lacked a certain polish.

Neale took the tune for 'Good King Wenceslas' unaltered
from the *Piae Cantiones*. The tune probably pre-dates the
book by about three hundred years. On this occasion, unlike
his other gleanings from the *Cantiones*, Neale chose not to
translate the original words. Easy to work out why. 'Tempus
adet floridum' is a secular song about spring. Another version
of this poem, from the *Carmina Burana* of the eleventh to
the thirteenth centuries, goes into rather more detail about
some of the activities traditionally associated with that time
of year, principally among priests and virgins, apparently.
Neale would have turned away a blushing eye.

It's a great tune. Elizabeth Poston thinks it sounds better
sung as intended, as an earthy spring song, stamping your
feet and playing the hurdy-gurdy. She has a point. The quirky
melisma in the last bar ('fu-u-el', etc.), which gives the last
line the wrong number of beats, sounds as if it is inviting the
singer to hurl his glass of schnapps skywards towards the
roof-tree. But, not for the first time, an English clergyman
decided to press a rambunctious old tune into the service of
higher things.

'Good King Wenceslas' is a song. Just another winter's tale. It may be only distantly related to Christmas, but it has the warm glow of a nice moral and a rousing tune, and it's snowing. That'll do. Our carols may not all turn out exactly as the grown-ups intended, but we can still love them for what they are.

'Good King Wenceslas'

Good King Wen-ces - las looked out on the feast of Ste - phen,

When the snow lay round a - bout, deep and crisp and e - ven.

Bright-ly shone the moon that night, though the frost was cru - el,

When a poor man came in sight, gath-'ring win-ter fu - el.

'Hither page and stand by me,
If thou know'st it, telling,
Yonder peasant, who is he?
Where and what his dwelling?'
'Sire, he lives a good league hence.
Underneath the mountain;
Right against the forest fence,
By Saint Agnes' fountain.'

'Bring me flesh, and bring me wine,
Bring me pine-logs hither:
Thou and I will see him dine,
When we bear them thither.'
Page and monarch forth they went,
Forth they went together;
Through the rude wind's wild lament,
And the bitter weather.

'Sire, the night is darker now,
And the wind blows stronger;
Fails my heart, I know now how,
I can go no longer.'
'Mark my footsteps, good my page;
Tread thou in them boldly;
Thou shalt find the winter's rage
Freeze thy blood less coldly.'

In his master's steps he trod,
Where the snow lay dinted;
Heat was in the very sod
Which the saint had printed.
Therefore, Christian men, be sure,
Wealth or rank possessing,
Ye who now will bless the poor,
Shall yourselves find blessing.

18

·: Personent hodie :·

PS: LXXXIX.

M*Isericordias* DO MI NI
in æternum cantabo, in gene-
ratione & generationem, annun-
ciabo veritatem tuam in ore meo.

t may appear slightly incongruous that one of the
principal sources of English Christmas carols
originated in Finland. The explanation lies in that
most potent force in the shaping of human destinies: luck.
The fact that this particular book survived, came into the
possession of a couple of English clergymen, who then used
it as a source for their own carol book, which in its turn
survived and prospered, is the result of a series of coinci-
dences and chance encounters.

There is no particular significance in the Finnish connection. There is no evidence that Father Christmas owned a copy, nor that it was nibbled by reindeer. This kind of song collection, mostly but not exclusively moral or devotional in character, was hugely popular in the European Renaissance period, part of the explosion of interest in education and ideals of behaviour, fuelled by the entrepreneurs of the new science of printing. There were thousands of such books. Most have vanished. Some will no doubt un-vanish: *Carmina Burana*, perhaps one thousand years old, lay undiscovered in a German monastery until the late nineteenth century. There are similar examples in all fields of music and literature. More are certainly waiting patiently to be excavated from library shelf and rood loft.

Singing is a Protestant habit. Like so many similar publications, *Piae Cantiones* begins with an earnest reminder that music exists to turn the mind 'ad cogitationem rerum divinarum' (or, as the contemporary Englishman Thomas Morley put it, 'to draw the hearer by the ears, as it were in chains of gold, to the consideration of holy things'). The Lutheran church put down deep and lasting roots in Scandinavia in the years around the publication of the *Piae Cantiones* in 1582. But at the time the old ways had not quite given up the ghost. Some of the texts are frankly Catholic in flavour, including two beautiful, tender settings of the 'Ave Maris Stella'.

Above all, it's a book of tunes. People like tunes. Suomalainen and his printer, Theodoric Petri of the district of Nyland, knew their market. Other editions followed, in Latin, Finnish and Swedish, new songs added along the way to maximise sales. They would surely have been thrilled, and probably rather astonished, to hear so many of their songs being lustily bellowed out by English carollers four centuries later, as a direct result of their book. Here are 'Gaudete', 'Resonet in laudibus', 'In dulci jubilo' (macaronic, but not as we know it, flitting fascinatingly between Latin and old Swedish), 'Puer nobis nascitur', 'Personent hodie', 'Tempus adet floridum' (which we know as 'Good King Wenceslas') and the tunes we sing as 'Up, Good Christen Folk and Listen' and 'Of the Father's Heart Begotten', among others. There is something thrilling about seeing these familiar tunes emerging from the square wooden type-face of Theodoric's press.

The book includes a few songs in two and four parts. There is a 'Passion' setting and some good Old Testament blood and thunder ('Judith fortis, Hester mortis'). It's the sort of musical mixture of practicality and piety which would have been instantly familiar to young men and maidens, old men and children, all over Protestant Europe.

Headmaster Suomalainen included some old favourites to get his pupils singing their little blond heads off. Like Luther and Calvin and their English outriders, the singing Finns pinched the best tunes they could find from the devil, the Pope, the pub and from nowhere in particular. 'Personent hodie' is probably one of the oldest, a good example of how a tune already weathered and seasoned by time made its way to Finland, on from there through the centuries to the choir stalls of Victorian England, and, eventually, to us. It is one of the very few carols we still regularly sing in Latin, and probably the oldest in which we sing tune and words as they were originally published together. Most of our carols consist of new words grafted onto old tunes, or vice versa, or both. Not this one.

The tune first appears in a written source in Germany in 1360, implying that it was already current then and thus probably of even older origin. Like others in the *Piae Cantiones*, the tune betrays its roots in the mediaeval dance-carol by a vigorous swagger that almost forces you to your feet to stamp the snow off your boots and freeze your blood less coldly. The gloriously wonky metrical pattern and rhyme scheme are unique and irresistible. Most striking is the repetition of a single syllable in line six ('et de vir-, vir-, vir-', etc).

The modern scholars Andrew Parrott and Hugh Keyte have an explanation for this engaging musical oddity. The text appears to be a version of an earlier poem in honour of St Nicholas, which begins 'Intonent hodie voces ecclesiae'. Nicholas, Bishop of Myra and the provinces, was also patron saint of children, and among other notable achievements brought back to life three boys who had drowned (or, depending which version you read, been murdered then pickled). In the interests of equality, Nicholas went on to rescue three girls from a life of prostitution. In the earlier text, the repeated syllable coincides with mentions of the lucky children ('submersum, -sum, -sum puerum', 'Reddens vir-, vir-, virginibus'). The three-fold repetition thus represents the three children each time. Perhaps there were some actions to go with it, a sort of mini-morality play or liturgical drama, or maybe a kind of counting-song.

The link with children survives in the 'voces puerulae' of the 1582 version. So does the repeated syllable, even though the immediate putative textual reason for it has been left behind. But note carefully what the page of music actually says at this point in the tune. The first appearance of the repeated syllable, *'et de vir-'*, has three repeated notes, as expected. The second, at the end of the line, quite clearly only has two. The syllable is sung first thrice, then twice, then once. Some later editors (but not all) changed it so that repetitions one and two are the same length, making a nice, regular little sequence. This is how we sing it today. Easier, maybe: but the tune has certainly lost some of its lopsided charm. (Note also that, rather sweetly, the printer has left out some of the words in the second verse, and someone has had to insert them over the top in pen.)

To find out how and why this wonderful melody has evolved and emigrated, the trail moves off-piste somewhat, to Stockholm and Queen Victoria's Minister in Residence, G. J. R. Gordon. By the 1850s, copies of the *Cantiones* were extremely rare. Gordon was presented with a copy which had belonged to Peter of Nyland, and in turn gave it to Neale and Helmore. They respectively edited and arranged the music,

'Personent hodie' from 'Piae Cantiones'

and translated or replaced the words. The result was two books, *Carols for Christmas-tide* of 1853, and *Carols for Easter-tide* of 1854. Each book contained twelve numbers, and the contents of both were later combined in a single, simplified version. European scholars worked on the *Cantiones* in the 1880s, and another English clergyman, George R. Woodward, produced an excellent edition of the whole book in 1910, using a kind of halfway notation combining the old square noteheads with modern clefs.

Their instinct for a good tune started the transfusion of much wonderful music into the blood-stream of the English carol singer. The title of the first published English version is significant. Neale and Helmore really did give us carols for 'Christmas-tide', not just for Christmas. We have already seen the (rather dodgy) link between 'Good King Wenceslas' and Boxing Day, 26 December. 'Personent hodie', with its evocation of children singing, has become associated with 28 December, the Feast of the Holy Innocents, and with the Epiphany, 6 January, where it fits with the tradition of St Nicholas bringing gifts to children on that day. We can still just catch the vinegary aroma of pickled boy hovering vaguely around this carol.

Neale also kicked off the favourite sport of coming up with English words for this tune. Poets and hymn writers have been unable to resist the challenge of finding rhymes to match the short lines and short syllables, and have had particular fun with the repeated word, or bit of word. Neale's own version begins (appropriately) 'Let the song be begun'. Holst's pupil Jane Marian Joseph published (under the pseudonym 'James M. Joseph') a well-known translation beginning 'On this day earth shall ring, with the song children sing, to the Lord, Christ our King'. Elizabeth Poston begins by rhyming at the half-line: 'Let the boys' cheerful noise', but soon gives it up: 'sing today none but joys'. Most translators cheat slightly at the end, treating the last few lines as a refrain, which they most certainly aren't in the original. Some even lapse pseudo-macaronically back into Latin at this point, which is perhaps to duck the issue.

Neale keeps the original number of appearances of the repetitious monosyllable:

Sing of joy, joy, joy,
Sing of joy, joy,
Earth and skies, Bid it rise,
Gloria in excelsis.

So does Woodward, in 1910:

Et de vir-, vir-, vir-,
Et de vir-, vir-,
Et de virgíneo ventre procreatus

Holst made a splendid arrangement in 1916 (sometimes known as 'Theodoric', taken by some authorities to be a reference to Holst's middle name, Theodore, but surely also a friendly nod to the printer of Hyland). The syllable has sprouted a sixth sibling:

Ide-o, -o, -o,
Ide-o, -o, -o,
Ideo Gloria in excelsis Deo

Joseph uses this same Latin refrain in her English version, complete with the spurious extra syllable stuck in the middle like a carrot on the face of a snowman.

F. Pratt Green's more recent version begins 'Long ago, prophets knew, Christ would come, born a Jew', and imaginatively turns the repeated syllable (including the spare) into a peal of bells:

Ring, bells, ring, ring, ring!
Sing, choirs, sing, sing, sing!
When he comes,
When he comes,
Who will make him welcome?

Piae Cantiones is a gem. We owe Neale and Helmore an incalculable debt for resurrecting these songs for us. Quite properly, they did so according to the mores of their age. We are perhaps entitled to begin to respectfully scrape off the Victorian varnish and re-discover this wonderful music for ourselves.

'Personent hodie'

Per - so - nent ho - di - e vo - ces pu - e - ru - lae, lau - dan - tes

iu - cun - de qui no - bis est na - tus, sum - mo De - o da - tus,

et de vir, vir, vir, et de vir, vir, et de

vir - gi - ne - o ven - tre pro - cre - a - tus.

In mundo nascitur,
pannis involvitur
praesepi ponitur
stabulo brutorum,
rector supernorum.
perdidit, -dit, -dit,
perdidit, -dit,
perdidit spolia princeps infernorum.

Magi tres venerunt,
parvulum inquirunt,
Bethlehem adeunt,
stellulam sequendo,
ipsum adorando,
aurum, thus, thus, thus,
aurum, thus, thus,
aurum, thus, et myrrham ei offerendo.

Omnes clericuli,
pariter pueri,
cantent ut angeli:
advenisti mundo,
laudes tibi fundo.
ideo, -o, -o,
ideo, -o,
ideo gloria in excelsis Deo.

19

·: Here We Come a-Wassailing :·

assail songs are probably the oldest, most numerous, most widespread and most varied of all our types of carol. Just as in the language itself, bits of Anglo-Saxon, Anglo-Norman, Anglo-Roman and Anglo-everything-else bob around in them like apples in a wassail cup. They are defiantly pagan, part fertility rite, part corporate village ritual: an incantation to the spirits of New Year and Old Twelfth Night.

Because there are so many wassail songs, separating out one individual for special attention is almost meaningless. It's like trying to spot a single tree in a vast, ancient forest.

The version given here only appears in this exact form late in the nineteenth century. But its imagery, its ideas and its rhythm, are part of a shared memory which goes back a millennium and more. Tracing some tiny part of this rich history can, perhaps, usefully be attempted by starting at the beginning of the poem, and, thus, more or less at the beginning of musical time.

'Here we come a-wassailing ... '

Here we come a-what? What is a wassail? And how do you come a-doing it?

The word itself is Old Norse in origin, found in Old English as 'Wæs Þu hæl'. It's a toast: 'be thou healthy'.

The response is 'Drinc hæl': the liquid components of this tradition were sloshed into the mix early. It probably pre-dates the arrival of Christianity in Northern Europe.

Writing in about 1140, Geoffrey of Monmouth has this account of the meeting in the fifth century between the warrior Vortigern and the maid Rowenne: 'flexis genibus lingua Saxonica ait "Washail, Lauert King"' ('bending her knee, she said in the Saxon language "Washail, Lord King"'). Vortigern, not understanding, is told: 'Your answer must be "Drinchail!"', and, 'from that time to this, it has been the custom in Britain, that he who drinks to anyone says "Washail!" and he that answers says "Drinchail!".' There are several accounts of this meeting. One refers to Britain as 'the land of Wassail and Drinchail'.

At the coronation of William of Normandy on Christmas Day 1066, his entourage cheered their new monarch in French, leading to a fight with the locals. Nearly a century later another new king, Henry II, and his glamorous queen, Eleanor of Aquitaine, were acclaimed in two languages, but this time it was Latin and Middle English: 'Ave Rex!' 'Wes hael!' English was fighting back.

In the early thirteenth century, this friendly bit of English good cheer made it into what is perhaps our very earliest written carol. Significantly, the phrase is dropped into a poem written in the formal language of court and law, Norman French (which is studded with Latinisms like 'quere' for 'seek'):

Seignors, ore entendez à nus,
De loinz sumes venuz à wous
Pur quere Noel …

    ... Si jo vus di trestoz, *Wesseyl!*
    Debaiz ait qui ne dirra *Drincheyl!*

Edith Rickert gives this translation:

    Lordings, listen to our lay-
    We have come from far away
    To seek Christmas...
    ... Here then I bid you all *Wassail,*
    Cursed be he who will not say *Drinkhail.*

' ... among the leaves so green ...'

Lots of carols take place outside. Why this one?

It's all to do with apples.

There is a ceremony which still persists in parts of Gloucestershire and elsewhere. It's called the Orchard-visiting Wassail. Groups of villagers are led by a Wassail king and queen to the orchard, drinking and singing as they go. The queen is lifted into the branches of the tree where she places a piece of toast soaked in a boozy apple-flavoured beverage. An incantation is recited, then the villagers make as much noise as they can, shouting and banging pots and pans together, until someone discharges a gun into the branches (making sure the queen has safely descended first), to chase away evil spirits and encourage the tree to produce a good harvest next year. Sometimes the drink is tipped down into the roots. Another variant is called 'howling', and involves whacking the tree with sticks.

Naturally, there are plenty of songs and rhymes to go with the ceremony, like this one:

    Old apple tree, we'll wassail thee,
    And hoping thou wilt bear.

The Lord does know where we shall be
To be merry anither year.

It's the sort of semi-theatrical, semi-pagan ritual which flourished before the Reformation. The authorities in the later sixteenth-century, businessmen as much as Puritans, preferred their artisans and journeymen to do their praying in church and spend the rest of the week working. In 1566, Fordwich in Kent owned a splendid set of costume 'appertaynyng to the kyng & the Quene of fordwiche'. In 1576, the town was told to end this 'superstycious or old custome … maynteyned vnder collour of boyes pastyme', and the 'apparell & other thinges of the late supposed kinge & Quene' were sold.

> ... here we come a-wandering,
> So fair to be seen,
> Love and joy come to you ...

Related to, but distinct from, the Orchard-visiting wassail is the House-visiting wassail. Villagers knock on their neighbours' door and offer to sing if they get food or money in return (or, depending on how you look at it, threaten to sing if they don't). The *Gentleman's Magazine* of 1791 relates how wassailers turn up at 'the house, the doors of which they are sure to find booted by the females, who, be the weather what it may, are inexorable to all entreaties to open them till some one has guessed at what is on the spit, which is generally some nice little thing, difficult to hit on, and is their reward of him who first names it. The doors are then thrown open, and the lucky clod pole receives the tit-bit as his recompense'.

... and to you your wassail too ...

As well as the greeting and the visiting ceremonies, the word 'wassail' also came to refer to the drink itself. It's made with apples, naturally enough, soused in a base of mulled mead or beer, spiced with sugar, ginger, nutmeg and cinnamon, heated and decanted into a specially made bowl with sops of toast floating on top. Yum.

Other recipes include roasted crab. A variety using baked apples is known as 'Lamb's Wool', as in Robert Herrick's poem 'Twelfth Night':

> Next crowne the bowle full
> With gentle Lambs wooll,
> Adde sugar, nutmeg, and ginger,
> With store of ale too,
> And thus ye must doe
> To make the Wassaile a swinger.

It sounds like this wassail was certainly going to be a 'swinger' (though it's interesting to speculate how, or whether, our sozzled carrolers made 'swinger' rhyme with 'ginger').

Needless to say, the name 'Lamb's Wool' defies explanation. It may be something to do with the pungent white froth exhaled by this particular brew. Others prefer to see it as a corruption of 'La Mas Ubhal', apple day, pronounced 'lamasool' and corrupted to 'lamb's wool'.

... and God bless you
And send you a Happy New Year ...

The refrain of our carol places it not at Christmas but at New Year. It takes its place alongside the Lords of Misrule, boy bishops, Twelfth Night revels and traditions of gift-giving loosely linked to the Three Kings. But there is far from unanimous agreement about which date is intended. Some use 1 January, others Twelfth Night, or the Eve of the Feast of the Epiphany (the end of Christmas), 5 January. But, when England (finally) switched from the Julian to the Gregorian Calendar in 1752, eleven days were missed out. Wednesday, 2 September 1752, was followed by Thursday, 14 September 1752, so that the day which fell exactly 365 days after Twelfth Night 1752 was called not 5 January 1753, but 17 January. Diehards thought that this was the 'true' Twelfth Night, and 17 January continues to be the favoured date for wassailling in many parts of the West Country, where it is known as 'Old Twelfth Night'.

... Our wassail cup is made
Of the rosemary tree ...

Here is yet another meaning for our little Anglo-Saxon word: the cup or bowl from which the 'wassail' drink is shared. It's large, round and made of some suitably flavourless native wood. This is from the 'Gloucestershire Wassail', nicely contrasting the colours of the various components:

> Wassail! wassail! all over the town,
> Our toast it is white and our ale it is brown;
> Our bowl it is made of the white maple tree;
> With the wassailing bowl, we'll drink to thee.

Maple sounds a better bet, on both flavour and carpentry grounds, than rosemary, which doesn't normally produce much in the way of timber.

More elaborate wassail cups are made in silver, like a

'loving cup'. Some have a spout, or several, so that when you drink from one you get drenched from another, which apparently adds to the fun.

At this point our modest little word takes on yet another shade of meaning. The Orchard-visiting wassail developed an indoor incarnation, where a plant or a small tree in a pot would be hung with decorated apples and the traditional pieces of doused toast. From here, tree decorations generally and baubles in particular become known as 'wessel cups'. The Yorkshire poet, Fred Hirst, born in 1917, has this:

> Ta decorate t' Christmas tree, we'd asked mi Mam
>   afooahr,
> This pahrticulahr time she couldn't stand it nooah
>   mooahr.
>
> She fetched it dahn from upstairs, Wessel cups an' all,
> On t' table she stood it; it wor abaht three feet tall.
>
> Silver tinsel, all ovver t' branches wo spread,
> Wessel cups wo gold, silver an' some wo red.

This usage is recorded all over Yorkshire. In Bradford it's 'Wesleybobs'.

Another local variant is the 'Gooding Carol', where the widows of the parish would go 'Gooding' or 'Thomasing' (or 'Tommying'), collecting alms on St Thomas's Day, 21 December, the shortest day of the year. The carol is also known as the 'Wessel Cup Carol'.

> ... We are not daily beggars
> That beg from door to door;
> But we are neighbours' children,
> Whom you have seen before ...

This carol is full of social protocol. The wassaillers are always keen to stress their status as neighbours, not the feared itinerant vagabonds, tinkers or minstrels, and thus stake their claim to the local squire's charity. Almost every version of this carol notes the social divide between the 'master' and the 'mistress' with their 'butler' wearing a 'golden ring', and the 'poor children ... wandering in the mire'.

Perhaps unsurprisingly, there are plenty of accounts of these encounters spilling over into confrontation or worse. 'We want a little of your money' can be sung as a benign request for pennies, or as something rather more sinister. Plenty of commentators have noticed that the practice of demanding goods with menaces has migrated into the imported American habit of 'trick-or-treat'.

Wassail songs are an interesting example of how the geographical spread of folk songs is linked to agriculture. This type of song grows best in the warm, hilly, rainy areas of the west and south-west of England, just like apples. Erik Routley notes that folk song, and folk carols in particular, are linked to farming areas. His 'folk song belt' runs diagonally across England from Cornwall to Yorkshire. Cumberland is 'no use at all'. It's partly cause and effect: there are lots of songs in the West Country, so Cecil Sharp went there, so we have lots of songs from the West Country. There's also an element of chance: Baring-Gould researched the 'Songs of the West' partly because he inherited an estate in Devon.

The prevalence of tunes (though not specifically carols) from Surrey, is, according to Routley, 'not unconnected with the fact that Dr Vaughan Williams lived many years at Dorking'.

Wassail songs come from everywhere. They are about everything: society, singing, dressing up, climbing trees, neighbourliness and not starving. They're about kings, queens and mouldy cheese. They are certainly about drinking. They encompass costumes, customs, songs, recipes, dances and decorations. The many varied spellings and renderings of the word itself hint at just how deep its associations go.

Above all, these songs are a celebration of life itself, of preservation and renewal.

God bless you, and Happy New Year.

'Here We Come a-Wassailing'

Here we come a was-sail-ing A-mong the leaves so green,
Here we come a wan-d'ring So fair to be seen. Love and joy come to
you, And to you your was-sail too, And God bless you and send you a
hap-py New Year, and God send you a hap-py New Year.

Our wassail cup is made
Of the rosemary tree,
And so is your beer
Of the best barley.
Refrain

We are not daily beggars
That beg from door to door,
But we are neighbours' children
Whom you have seen before.
Refrain

Good Master and good Mistress,
As you sit by the fire,
Pray think of us poor children
Are wandering in the mire.
Refrain

We have a little purse
Made of ratching leather skin;
We want some of your small change
To line it well within.
Refrain

Call up the Butler of this house,
Put on his golden ring;
Let him bring us a glass of beer,
And the better we shall sing.
Refrain

Bring us out a table,
And spread it with a cloth;
Bring us out a mouldy cheese,
And some of your Christmas loaf.
Refrain

God bless the Master of this house,
Likewise the Mistress too;
And all the little children
That round the table go.
Refrain

('ratching' is leather which will stretch)

20

·: The Twelve Days of Christmas :·

hall we make the welkin dance indeed? Shall we rouse the night-owl … ?'

Shakespeare knew all about Twelfth Night. His play is basically one long party. Sir Toby Belch and Sir Andrew Aguecheek are the Lords of Misrule, the descendants of the midwinter household gods of the Roman, of Bacchus and Terpsichore.

'On the twelfth day of December!' bellows Sir Toby, as muddled about what day it is as he is about the time of night.

Would we have recognised his tune to these words?

Twelfth Night had long been one of the principal festivities of the Christmas season. At the court of Henry VIII it far outdid Christmas Day as a household knees-up, with masques, dances, morality plays with songs and scenery, and gift-giving echoing the shadowy presence, somewhere off-stage, in the wings, of the shades of wise men and St Nicholas. Sir Toby quotes 'Three merry men be we', a song no doubt well-known to the boozy groundlings, evoking the 'three-men's songs' (or 'freemen's songs') of early Tudor song books. Party songs: rough, carefree, designed to sound better sung drunk.

But Shakespeare is writing in the death throes of this festive tradition. There is something desperate and sad in

Sir Andrew and Sir Toby's manic partying, as if trying to keep something at bay: "'tis too late to go to bed now'. It is significant that when Malvolio tries to make them shut up, Sir Toby spits at him that he's 'a puritan'. This kind of midwinter merry-making is on the way out. The theatre itself, the 'great globe', is under attack. Our revels now are ended.

But something of the generous spirit of the twelve day holiday survives in this sprightly carol, even if nowadays we do Christmas in the wrong order. We put our decorations up and file dutifully into our carol services during Advent, or even earlier. Christmas effectively ends, rather than begins, on 25 December. In earlier days, and still in many traditions, gifts are given on Boxing Day, or through to the twelfth day of Christmas. This is the spirit still captured in this song. Twelfth Night, for us, is the day decorations come down (if they haven't already fallen behind the TV), the day we sweep up pine needles and broken bits of bauble and try to pretend the days are getting longer. Herrick, in the seventeenth century, talks of household decorations of holly and yew coming down at Candlemas, 2 February, when the infant Jesus was presented to the world.

Christmas carols cover many different seasonal festivities and come in many different types. 'The Twelve Days of Christmas' is a 'numeral' carol, itself a sub-set of a species of folk song, counting songs.

There are lots of these (count them): 'Green grow the rushes-oh'; 'Ten green bottles'; 'Five little monkeys'; 'One man went to mow'; 'This old man'; 'One, two, buckle my shoe', 'One, two, three, four, five, once I caught a fish-alive', 'Ten in a bed', 'One potato, two potato', etc. Some count down, some up. Some are in dialect, like 'Yan, tan, tethera, methera, pimp', Cumbrian words for one, two, three, four, five. Cumulative rhymes with a similar structure include 'This is the house that Jack built'; 'There was an old woman who swallowed a fly'; 'My gran went to market', and countless others.

They're games. You can sing them in the playground, walking down the street, or on a boring bus journey. You can use them as 'forfeit' games, where the first person to stumble over the ever-growing list of goodies has to drop out, or give someone a treat or a kiss. They're inclusive: any number of people can join in. They're good for concentration and teamwork, and they also, of course, help teach young children to count, forwards or backwards (or both), sometimes with an element of spelling or linguistics thrown in (where the objects accumulate in alphabetical or some other order).

Religion uses numbers in its imagery a lot. There are three ships, three kings, three persons, four evangelists, ten commandments and twelve disciples. There are obvious possibilities for counting-songs with a devotional tinge.

'Green grow the rushes' places the four 'gospel-makers' alongside the 'lily-white boys, clothed all in green', as if both are figures carved into English mythology, as indeed they are, like the Green Man grinning incongruously at us from many a church corbel and plinth, impishly eye-balling a worried-looking saint or virgin on the next pillar along. The four evangelists appear again in the haunting 'Matthew, Mark, Luke and John, bless the bed that I lie on'. The 'seven joys' of Mary make a gorgeous song. In other versions her joys are ten, or five, or twelve. There are twelve apostles, twelve months of the year, twelve 'points' and twelve articles.

CHRISTMAS CAROLS

Gifts given over a twelve-day period clearly fit this kind of song perfectly.

The song, in turn, lends itself to infinite local adaptation. There are versions from Alabama ('ten mules braying'), New England ('guns shooting, bears chasing, men hunting'), Scotland ('goldspinks, plovers, and a papingo-aye'), and many other invasive species. Even within England the gifts and their order keep changing. In the very many versions found between 1780 and 1909, the first seven gifts stay pretty much the same (with the notable exception of the 'calling-birds', which are, variously, collie, colley, colly, Corley, curley, coloured and canary birds, most of which are terms for a blackbird). One version has 'squabs a-swimming' instead of swans, which are baby pigeons and can't swim. From verse eight upwards singers swap, substitute and generally muddle up the rest of the gifts, including 'boys a-singing', 'ships a-sailing', 'lads a-louping' instead of 'lords a-leaping', 'hounds a-running' and 'badgers baiting'.

Much analysis has gone into the symbolism of all of this, perhaps sometimes searching for meaning which may actually not be there. It might really just be a list of things seen around the farmhouse and the village.

None of the gifts has received such attention as the first. Is the dumpy little partridge part of the aviary of mediaeval icons which includes the 'soft, self-wounding pelican' and 'the carnal and the crane'? If so, why is it in a tree? The RSPB informs us that this is 'strictly a ground bird, never likely to be found in pear trees'.

Here is one attractive possible explanation. The best early source of this song is a little children's song book called 'Mirth without mischief', printed in 1780. The words are much as we know them today.

Across the Channel there is a popular *chanson enfantine* called 'Les douze mois de l'année'. The song has the same cumulative structure and a rhythmically similar melody to its English *confrère*, the gifts, interestingly, spread over the twelve months of the year rather than the twelve days of Christmas: 'deux tourterelles, trois ramiers au bois', up to 'onze beaux garçons' and 'douze demoiselles gentilles et belles'.

A brief etymological diversion. According to Greek mythology, the first partridge was created when Daedalus threw his nephew off a tower. The nephew was called Perdix. The ornithological name for the Grey Partridge is *Perdix perdix*. The French derivation from this is *perdrix*. The alternative name for our children's song is 'La Perdriole', 'The little partridge'.

We have our pear tree. It's a *perdrix*. It's a half-remembered mis-translation, or, perhaps, a mis-remembered half-translation, giving us, oddly, not one partridge up a tree, but two, both on the ground. One English, one French. A partridge *et un perdrix*.

Voilà.

Here's another intriguing possibility. At least one version has as the first gift not the familiar partridge, but 'part of a juniper tree'. Look how closely the syllables of the two alternative lines, vowels and consonants, match up:

```
And a part-ri-i-dge in a   pear tree
And a part of a      ju-ni-per  tree
```

Given the way an oral tradition works, it is entirely

The partridge, from 'Mirth without mischief', 1780

plausible that one is a garbled version of the other. If so, which is the original? Juniper has its ancient and hallowed place among traditional decorative midwinter greenery. Perhaps it came first. Someone heard it wrong, sang it back as a partridge, everyone laughed, and it stuck. It's a mistake, a happy accident by an inattentive toddler or a deaf grandma.

Sometimes we have 'a merry partridge in the barley', probably a more sensible place for it to forage and roost. There are many, many other versions.

Like the little 1780 book, most printed versions don't include a melody. Unsurprisingly, folk-song collectors found it sung to a whole host of tunes round the country, from Devon to Northumbria and beyond. Cecil Sharp alone noted at least seven. Some are clearly related, others are distinct items in their own right.

One thing most of the tunes have in common is that 'five gold rings' (or 'golden rings', or 'five, a golden ring') is sung to the same snatch of melody as all the other gifts from five up. Our little flourish and *fermata* at this point is a later addition.

Step forward a middleweight Wagnerian baritone and minor composer, Frederick Austin. 'Minor' is right. No composer has ever achieved so many worldwide performances over such a long period from such a small surviving output: four notes.

Austin was a musician of some substance. He sang Elgar for Elgar and Schoenberg to Schoenberg. He sang in Beecham's *Ring* and Richter's *Tannhäuser*. He premiered works by composers from Cyril Scott to Vaughan Williams. He edited *The Beggar's Opera*. Henry Wood, who conducted Austin's symphonic 'Rhapsody', said that Austin was the only man who could sing Delius's *Sea Drift 'con amore'*.

In 1909 Austin published an arrangement of 'The Twelve Days of Christmas'. In it, he added his own little phrase at 'five gold rings', ornamenting the last appearance with a twiddly little cadenza of the sort he no doubt sang himself, *con amore*, around the piano at Edwardian *soirées*. His version, sans cadenza, stuck in the public mind. Austin gave us the song we know today (and, in the process, gave us the small problem of a non-copyright folk song with four copyright notes stuck in the middle). He also regularised a couple of other details which have since become standard: the first word, 'on', where earlier versions began simply 'The first day of Christmas', etc.; and 'calling' birds instead of the various types of blackbird. Unlike the 'rings', however, in these instances it seems possible that was just noting down what people usually sang, rather than adding something of his own.

Much could be written about the infinite variety of musical structure within the narrow confines of the little tunes in this book. This one has a curious cumulative shape, where gifts two to four at first get the same melodic hook, but only until the presentation of gift five, after which they each get a new tune of their own and gifts six and upwards get the original melodic fragment. It's an odd way to put together a melody, but very satisfying.

In most versions the gifts are handed over from one to twelve, in some the other way round, occasionally both, forwards then backwards. Almost all the tunes put the opening and closing 'refrain' in 4/4 and switch to some kind of triple time for the recitation of the gifts, adding a rushing, helter-skelter excitement to the playground memory test.

Some didn't get it. A humourless public-school type of 1869 sniffed at 'its peculiarity and the utter absurdity of the words', which of course completely misses the point. Nonsense songs are supposed to be nonsense. Recent wits have had fun pretending to take it literally. John Julius Norwich has composed a set of letters from the recipient to the true love, beginning with delighted surprise and ending with the donor being arrested for stalking. The notional value of the total basket of gifts is used as a light-hearted measure of seasonal prices ($114,651.18 in 2013, apparently, up a worrying 7.7 per cent on the year before, assuming minimum wage for the milkmaids, union rates for drummers and pipers and quotes from reputable aviaries, jewellers and garden centres).

And so we reach the twelfth day. This is the Christmas of revels, of parties and gifts. And somewhere under the happy surface of this little song lurks the ancient spirit of Twelfth Night.

'The Twelve Days of Christmas'

2

true love sent to me   five gold rings,   four calling birds,

three French hens, two turtle doves, and a partridge in a pear tree.   On the

(add a bar each time)

sixth day of Christmas my true love sent to me   six geese a-laying,
seventh   seven swans a-swimming,
eighth   eight maids a-milking,
ninth   nine ladies dancing,
tenth   ten lords a-leaping,
eleventh   eleven pipers piping,
twelfth   twelve drummers drumming,

five gold rings,   four calling birds,   three French hens,

two turtle doves, and a partridge in a pear tree.

21

·: We Three Kings :·

everal of our best-loved carols are American. The United States has its own distinctive traditions about how and where to do carols. The Christmas pageant is the equivalent of what the British call a nativity play. Both are directly descended from, and closely related to, the mediaeval liturgical drama and mystery play.

Its grown-up cousin, the Christmas Parade, is a sort of ancient Roman victory march in Santa hats, a kind of Christmas ticker-tape parade, all sequins, songs and civic pride, with a strong dash of commercialism thrown in. Hollywood hovers like a presiding angel. 'We Three Kings' owes something to this semi-theatrical tradition.

John Henry Hopkins Jr. was a clergyman. He worked initially in journalism and the law before studying for ordination at the General Theological Seminary in New York City, graduating in 1850. Five years later he took up the post of music teacher at his old college, combining it with his ministry as rector of Christ Episcopal Church in nearby Williamsport, Pennsylvania. 'We Three Kings' was written for a pageant at the seminary in 1857, and published with a number of his other Christmas pieces in *Carols, Hymns and Songs* in 1863.

Like its close cousin 'Away in a Manger', 'We Three Kings' is a performance piece. An element of staging, actual or implied, is built into the structure. The first and last verses, and the intervening refrains, are in harmony, a universal hymn of praise. Verses two, three and four are each given to one of the 'kings', presenting his gift and commenting on its symbolic significance. These verses can be sung by three soloists, and Hopkins tells us with all the pragmatism of the music teacher: 'men's voices are best for the parts of the Three Kings, but the music is set in the G clef for the accommodation of children'. Performers can move around the church or hall, stopping for each verse and journeying on towards the crib during the refrains in a version of the mediaeval 'stations' (the word is related to 'stanza'). This is exactly like the very earliest liturgical dramas such as the Easter *'Quem quaeritis'* ('whom seek ye?'), where individual members of the choir would take the roles of the angel and the three Marys and 'act out' the gospel stories in music, hiding behind an altar or pillar and popping out when the stone is rolled away.

Hopkins's tune is in the 'Aeolian mode', an appropriately Eastern-sounding musical scale, much remarked upon and occasionally mistaken for a genuine folk song. His words are powerful and direct, at their best when repetition and simplicity of language evoke the swinging, purposeful march towards Bethlehem ('Star of wonder, star of light, star with royal beauty bright').

It's an effective and unusual conception. It's also one of a tiny number of our carols where we know for certain that words and music are by the same person, who he was and what he wrote. Naturally, this hasn't stopped editors and compilers fiddling around with it.

Why is this still acceptable for hymns, when the whole

thrust of modern editorial and scholarly good practice is to try to get as close as possible to an 'authentic' version of what author or composer intended? Hopkins didn't like it any more than John Wesley did a century earlier. It brought out the lawyer in him: 'Compilers of other Collections are at liberty to transfer any of the pieces in this little volume, provided they leave what they take unaltered. If any change be made in either words or music without my permission, I shall prosecute the offender to the extent of the law.' It didn't work, of course.

The hymns in Hopkins's 'little volume' cover a range of Christmas themes. By writing about the characters he called the 'Three Kings of Orient' he was entering the much-stirred waters of debate about whether they were kings, and whether there were three of them.

It doesn't matter. Scripture doesn't say they were, but it doesn't say they weren't. 'Kings' is a convenient shorthand for educated aristocrats. Anyway, nineteenth-century Americans were supposed to be unbothered about the niceties of noble rank and titles (notwithstanding the observations of Dickens and Henry James). As for their number, the other kings might just be off in the wings, unpacking the odours of Edom or checking the gold of obedience for dents.

Hopkins had hit on something. This carol stood out. It made it into many published collections, not all of them heeding his lawyerly instructions about leaving the text 'unaltered'.

Henry Ramsden Bramley and John Stainer brought it to England in their *Christmas Carols New and Old* of 1878. Between the great carol-collectors of the mid nineteenth century (Sandys, Husk, Sylvester, etc.) and the folklorists of the turn of the twentieth (Sharp, Baring-Gould, Vaughan Williams), the compilers of the first carol books for choirs are among the heroes of this story. Their job was to provide something people would want to use. The repertoire we know today was to a large extent assembled and codified by them. Bramley and Stainer were among the first, most serious, most musical and best of the arranger-editors. These two kings of carolling are the great-grand-daddies of the 'University' carol books, the 'Cowley' carol book and every similar collection since.

The 'three kings' and their carol have had their fair share of parody, perhaps because, like the shepherds with their socks, they are not part of the Holy Family or celestial choir, which makes them fair game. In the story, they represent us, so we can share a joke with them.

Very young children can still quite easily be reduced to helpless giggles by songs of the

> We Three Kings of Orient are
> One in a taxi, one in a car,
> One on a scooter, tooting his hooter,
> Eating a chocolate bar.

variety.

A Christmas sermon might begin with an account of a nativity play, like this one:

> The first king steps forward and says, 'Gold'.
>   'Myrrh', proclaims the second.
>   The third strides to the front of the stage and announces, 'Frank sent this'.

The American pageant and parade created a distinctive subset of Christmas songs. Theatrical, colourful and inclusive, they lead directly into the world of 'Jingle Bells', and the Irving Berlin of 'White Christmas' and 'Easter Parade'. These are secular, seasonal party-songs. This is what carols were for before they involved the sacred.

Hopkins gets his kings to reflect for us on the whole of the message of Christ's coming, from their summoning by the star to the symbolic presence of the 'stone-cold tomb'. He picks up some very ancient themes. The 'Carol of the Star' is one of our oldest written carols. Folk carols like the 'Cherry Tree' and the 'Dancing Day' embrace the whole Christian worldview from Christmas to Easter, as Hopkins does.

The 'star of wonder' has been guiding poets and musicians to its perfect light for a long time.

'We Three Kings'

Caspar:
Born a King on Bethlehem plain,
Gold I bring to crown Him again,
King forever,
Ceasing never
Over us all to reign.
Refrain

Melchior:
Frankincense to offer have I;
Incense owns a Deity nigh:
Prayer and praising
All men raising,
Worship Him God on high.
Refrain

Balthazar:
Myrrh is mine; it's bitter perfume;
Breathes a life of gathering gloom: —
Sorrowing, sighing,
Bleeding, dying,
Sealed in the stone-cold tomb.
Refrain

All:
Glorious now behold Him arise,
King and God and sacrifice.
Heav'n sings Hallelujah;
Hallelujah the earth replies.
Refrain

·: What Child is This? :·

et the sky rain potatoes! Let it thunder to the tune of "Green Sleeves"!'

Shakespeare mentions 'Greensleeves' twice in *The Merry Wives of Windsor*. The other mention has nothing to do with potatoes:

> I shall think the worse of fat men, as long as I have an eye to make difference of men's liking. And yet he would not swear; praised women's modesty; and gave such orderly and well-behaved reproof to all uncomeliness, that I would have sworn his disposition would have gone to the truth of his words: but they do no more adhere and keep pace together, than the Hundredth Psalm to the tune of Green Sleeves.

There are two points of interest here. The first is that 'Greensleeves' was obviously well enough known by around 1597, when Shakespeare wrote this play (apparently at the personal request of the Queen, who wanted more of her favourite fat man, Falstaff), for him to name-check it and expect his audience to get the reference. The second is that even by that date people were singing this tune with all sorts of words. Mistress Ford is referring to the practice of using folk songs, or any other kind of well-known tune, to sing metrical versions of the psalms (that is, rhyming and in a regular metre). The practice was widespread from the mid sixteenth century, and it's no surprise to find 'Greensleeves' being recruited for this purpose.

This is the tradition to which William Chatterton Dix and John Stainer were contributing when they made the tune of Green Sleeves adhere and keep place together with the poem 'What Child is This?' in the late nineteenth century.

Before it got to that point, this lovely little tune had plenty of other words sung to it. William Chappell made a methodical study of its origins and use in his 'Popular music of the olden time' of 1859. Chappell was the father of musical antiquarianism, and still one of the best. He tells us that 'Greensleeves' was first recorded in 1580, already popular and therefore certainly much older. Although he thinks it 'must be a tune of Henry's reign', he certainly didn't set running the old hare that 'Henry' wrote it. He didn't.

Thereafter, the tune was regularly pressed into service to make a political or religious point, often by both sides of an argument at the same time. There are songs for and against Puritans, Catholics, Oliver Cromwell and the Jacobites. There is even a splendidly scurrilous song about attempts to cover up the fact that the Pope had become a father.

On one occasion it had words sung to it to accompany an execution:

You traitors all that do devise
To hurt our Queen in treacherous wise,
And in your hearts do still surmise
Which way to hurt our England;
Consider what the end will be
Of traitors all in their degree:

Hanging is still their destiny
That trouble the peace of England.

Chappell notes that 'The conspirators were treated with very little consideration by the ballad monger in having their exit chaunted to a merry tune, instead of the usual lamentation', which may perhaps have been the least of their worries at the time.

Like all good folk songs, 'Greensleeves' could simultaneously lend itself to this sort of street-level stuff and to the proprieties of divine worship without batting an eyelid. As early as 1580, Chappell finds 'Greene Sleves moralised to the Scripture, declaring the manifold benefites and blessings of God bestowed on sinful man', exactly the sort of thing Mistress Ford, and Stainer and Dix, had in mind.

The carol tradition appeared early in the encyclopaedia of texts associated with this flexible and beautiful tune. One song, for harvest, says 'a pie sat on a pear-tree top', a curious echo of both the apple-wassail carols and 'The Twelve Days of Christmas'.

'A Carol for New Year's Day, to the tune of Green Sleeves' was printed in a ballad sheet in 1642. It is perhaps worth quoting in full:

The old year now away is fled,
The new year it is entered;
Then let us now our sins down tread,
And joyfully all appear.
Let's merry be this holiday,
And let us run with sport and play,
Hang sorrow, let's cast care away –
God send you a happy new year.

And now with new year's gifts each friend
Unto each other they do send;
God grant we may our lives amend,
And that the truth may appear.
Now like the snake cast off your skin
Of evil thoughts and wicked sin
And to amend this new year begin –
God send us a merry new year.

And now let all the company
In friendly manner all agree,
For we are here welcome all may see
Unto this jolly good cheer.
I thank my master and my dame,
The which are founders of the same,
To eat to drink now is no shame –
God send us a merry new year.

Come lads and lasses every one,
Jack, Tom, Dick, Bess, Mary, and Joan,
Let's cut the meat unto the bone,
For welcome you need not fear.
And here for good liquor we shall not lack,
It will whet my brains and strengthen my back,
This jolly good cheer it must go to wrack –
God send us a merry new year.

Come, give us more liquor when I do call,
I'll drink to each one in this hall,
I hope that so loud I must not bawl,
But unto me lend an ear.
Good fortune to my master send,
And to my dame which is our friend,
God bless us all, and so I end –
And God send us a happy new year.

We are back where we started. This is the carol as celebration and a celebration of the carol, hymning the virtues of the village and its hierarchy, with plenty of folk religion thrown in (like the image of sin as the skin of a snake, a flesh-creeping image worthy of the mediaeval 'doom' painters), and a respectful doff of the cap to the Christian God tacked on the end, almost as an afterthought, as if the squire has just strolled stoutly by, roasted capon-leg in one hand, flagon of ale in the other.

This ballad dates from just before the Puritans launched their all-out assault on this sort of 'jolly good cheer'. By the time the creators of 'What Child is This?' joined the noble tradition two centuries later, things had calmed down a bit.

William Chatterton Dix was an insurance salesman. His father was a doctor and a big fan of the poet, forger, and the romantic period's favourite suicide, Thomas Chatterton. Dix senior wrote a biography of Chatterton and gave young William a florid combination of his own and his subject's names. This upbringing in a devout, intensely literary but commercially astute family led Chatterton Dix into the twin preoccupations of his life: marine insurance and writing hymns.

He was an excellent hymn writer. This is from another Christmas lyric, 'The Manger Throne':

> The stars of heaven still shine as at first
> They gleamed on this wonderful night;
> The bells of the city of God peal out
> And the angels' song still rings in the height,
> And love still turns where the Godhead burns
> Hid in flesh from fleshly sight.

> Faith sees no longer the stable floor,
> The pavement of sapphire is there
> The clear light of heaven streams out to the world
> And the angels of God are crowding the air,
> And heaven and earth through the spotless birth
> Are at peace on this night so fair.

Note the subtle internal rhyme in the middle of line five. This hymn, alas for Dix, got itself hitched to a typically purple tune by Joseph Barnby, and never quite recovered. Some of his other poems were more lucky. 'As with Gladness' found itself a nice tune (which its arranger called 'Dix', which is rather sweet), and has lived happily with it ever since.

Dix wrote 'What Child is This?' in about 1865. It first appeared to the tune 'Greensleeves' in Bramley and Stainer's *Christmas Carols New and Old* in 1871.

There is no suggestion that Dix intended his words for this tune. He may possibly have had another tune in mind. More likely not. His many books of devotional verse have titles like *Altar Songs* and *Hymns of Love and Joy*, which imply singing, but don't specify a tune. Like the compiler of Mistress Ford's psalm book, he was content to leave the choice of melody up to his singers. In this case, like Mistress Ford, they reached for their old favourite 'Greensleeves'. The words don't fit terribly well. But then, the tune has some fluid and unexpected little twists of shape and rhythm which have defeated other wordsmiths, balladeers and professional hymnologists alike. It's that very unexpectedness which makes it such a ravishing tune.

It's also what makes it so hard to pin down. Like all real folk songs, there is no 'correct' version. Editors and arrangers can't agree whether the sixth degree of the scale is raised or lowered and which pairs of quavers are dotted and which aren't. It's all part of the rich joy of the folk song. The marriage of tune and words was inspired. It was probably Stainer's idea. It wasn't perhaps the most obvious match, but it worked. The wise men are given the privilege of following the star and revealing the message of Christmas to the world, and the quiet rapture of an English folk-song is given the privilege of revealing their message to us.

What better place to leave, for now, the story of the English carol.

'What Child Is This'

What child is this, who, laid to rest, on Mary's lap is sleep-ing, Whom an-gels greet with an-thems sweet, while shep-herds watch are keep-ing? This, this is Christ the King, whom shep-herds praise and an-gels sing: Haste, haste to bring him praise, Je-sus the son of Ma-ry.

How comes He in such mean estate,
Where ox and ass are feeding?
Yet have no fear, God's love is here,
His love all loves exceeding.
Raise, raise your song on high,
As Mary sings a lullaby.
See, see, where Christ is born,
Jesus the Son of Mary.

Earth, give Him incense, gold and myrrh,
Come, tribes and people, own Him;
The King of kings salvation brings,
So in your hearts enthrone Him.
Nails, spear shall pierce Him through,
Such pain he bore for me and you.
Praise, praise, the Son of Man,
Jesus the Son of Mary.

·: Epilogue :·

he glory days of the English carol tradition were the dark, ancient times of dances round the fire and festivals of cakes and ale. Congregational singing, beginning in the sixteenth century with the Reformation, led eventually to the carol being allowed inside the church, and to the distinctive sound of the eighteenth-century Christmas, a sort of mixture of folk music and Handel. Nineteenth-century clerics played a crucial role, writing and translating a large chunk of our repertoire, and unearthing and arranging all kinds of Christmas melodies from ages past. Their high-church, Anglo-Catholic style was hugely influential, embracing not just traditional carols, many of which might otherwise have remained hidden, but hymns, ancient and modern, and plainsong. They invented the tub-thumper, the pot-boiler and the descant. They rediscovered modes and draped them with the beauty of holiness and the dominant thirteenth. They did for mediaeval music what Gilbert Scott did for Gothic architecture and Tennyson did for the legend of King Arthur: Victorianised it, but saved it. It's all a bit 'Merrie England'. Amis's Lucky Jim would have recognised it. In some ways they were the Henry Higgins of the English choral tradition, scrubbing away all traces of the accent of the street or the field.

They also invented the carol service. Pioneered (in a

Cornish shed) by that most muscular of muscular Christians, Bishop E. W. Benson, and his Dean, Eric Milner-White, the carol service has become so much part of our heritage that it's easy to forget just what a novel, and relatively recent creature it is. Earlier generations would have been shocked to find these songs, the illegitimate offspring of Western Christianity and a naughty ploughboy, with their muddy knees and earthy language, at the heart of divine worship, in an actual liturgy, a church service, in church. Good King Wenceslas used to look in, not out.

One result of welcoming them inside is that we have rather smoothed over the difference between folk carols and ecclesiastical hymns. But the difference is striking. Look closely, and the lurch from one to the other is like coming into the cool, carved interior of a church from the open fields outside, or, as Routley put it, 'like approaching Wolverhampton from the north by train'. Hymns are about what happens in the Bible, with a devotional point attached. Somebody wrote them. Carols are about pretty much anything at all, except, usually, what happens in the Bible. Nobody wrote them.

Twentieth-century composers saw the rich expressive potential of the old texts and started making new settings, often incorporating the sound-world of modal harmony and folk song, and the 'stanza and burden' structure of the folk carol. The 'carol-anthem' is born. They made arrangements and quasi-symphonic suites of the old tunes in their own musical style, too, sometimes, like those of Vaughan Williams, quite extended. Compositions and arrangements begin to sound rather alike. Poets like William Morris and Christina Rossetti wrote effective new carol texts in a deliberately archaic style. Musicians also learned to mine the poetry of the seventeenth and eighteenth centuries, of Herbert, Godolphin, Wither, Wesley and Watts, with some gorgeous results. Benjamin Britten, in particular, found a rich vein of inspiration in the early English carol texts included by Sir Arthur Quiller-Couch in the influential *Oxford Book of English Verse* of 1900.

Later twentieth-century composers started to set brand-new poetry in their carols, sometimes specially written, like Bruce Blunt and Peter Warlock composing 'Bethlehem Down' as payment to the landlord of a pub for a bar-bill they couldn't afford.

The next stroke of genius was 'art'-carols with the virtues of the best pop and show tunes. Simplicity with something to say is the hardest thing a composer can try to do. Words have an appropriately old-world feel. The best of the melodies have the same innate feel for Sharp's 'unconscious art' of the folk singer as the best of Dylan or Lennon and McCartney. Harmonies might not always pass the Vaughan Williams test for the avoidance of Victorian sentimentality: the whiff of Gounod occasionally wafts from the page like incense swung from a rattling censer by a lacy little altar-boy.

But the composed, 'art' tradition of carols for trained choirs is not our subject here, though it draws heavily on community and folk carol singing, with sophisticated, subtle and beautiful results.

Where now? Is the oral tradition over? Our farm-boy does not now follow the plough, whistling his local variant of 'While Shepherds Watched'. His team is not now ploughing in summertime on Bredon. He doesn't chase a mouse down a hole, cheerfully singing 'I'll give you one-oh' as he whacks it with a stick. But he does use his mouse to listen to music from all over the world. Vaughan Williams and Cecil Sharp feared that recording, mass media and the electronic age would kill off local traditions, because everyone would have instant access to the same things. Like all prophets of technological doom, they were partly right. There are fewer variants of 'While Shepherds Watched' sung today, but there are still some. Local variation, fascinatingly, is between countries, not villages – between Britain and America, or England and Scotland – and between religious denominations.

And, as well as potentially reducing local variety, recording and the internet have of course opened up for us the musical resources of the whole world. An English carol service may very well already contain indigenous songs from Poland, the Basque country, the Appalachians, or Spain. Who knows what might be next? Tinselly English Christmas carols are enormously popular in China. Christianity has been well established in India, Japan and elsewhere for many centuries now. Where are their songs? Where is the version of the Nativity with the water-buffalo and the wildebeest? Or some beautiful, lilting raga of lullaby to the Christ-child? Somebody, soon, will have huge fun finding the African or Indian or Inuit equivalent of 'Riu, riu' or 'Patapan' or 'I wonder as I wander' and arranging their visa to the English choir stall. There's lots more music out there waiting to be welcomed in to the wassail.

And besides, we haven't finished with our own songs yet. We have tapped the researches of Cecil Sharp and others in the south of England pretty thoroughly, but we have hardly started on the work of collectors like Marjorie Kennedy-Fraser in the Western Isles of Scotland. There are treasures there.

The Vindication of
CHRISTMAS,
OR,
His Twelve Yeares Observations upon the

Times, concerning the lamentable Game called Sweep-
stake ; acted by General *Plunder*, and Major General *Tax*;
With his Exhortation to the people ; a description of that
oppressing Ringworm called *Excise* ; and the manner how
our high and mighty Christmas-Ale that formerly would
knock down *Hercules*, & trip up the heels of a Giant, strook
into a deep Consumption with a blow from *Westminster*.

Imprinted at London for G. Horton, 1653.

And have the carols we do have stopped evolving? Have we decided whether to sing a passing-note at 'born the King of a-a-angels' or not? We have not.

There's plenty more evolving left to do. And plenty more singing.

Pass the mince pies.

Happy Christmas.

∴ List of Illustrations ∴

·: Notes on the CD :·

 CD is available as a companion to this book. It takes the same journey through the Christmas season and the history of the carol as the book, but doesn't always stop at exactly the same places. Thus we get just a small hint of the variety and flexibility of the tradition, and the shining throng of tunes and texts it has folded within its wings. Carols are sung in versions you will know and versions you won't, and sometimes both. Some of the tunes you will recognise from somewhere completely different. Musical arrangements cover probably about half a millennium.

Track listing:
1. The Angel Gabriel (Basque trad., tr. Baring-Gould, arr. Gant)
2. Veni, veni, Emmanuel (arr. Helmore/Gant, tr. Neale/Lacey)
3. O Tannenbaum (German; harmony from the 'Yale song book')
4. The Holly and the Ivy (English trad., arr. Walford Davies)
5. I Saw Three Ships (English trad., arr. Gant)
6. O Little Town of Bethlehem (English trad., arr. Vaughan Williams; descant: Armstrong. Text: Brooks)
7. In dulci jubilo (German, arr. Thiel)
8. Adeste, fideles (eighteenth century)

9. Whilst Shepherds Watched (Music: 'Winchester Old',
    c. 1592, vv. 3 and 4 arr. Ravenscroft. Text: Tate)
10. The Fleecy Care (English trad.)
11. Whilst Shepherds Watched (Music: 'Cranbrook', Clark.
    Text: Tate)
12. Ding Dong! Merrily on High (French, arr. Tabourot/Wood.
    Text: Woodward)
13. Célébrons la naissance (French, arr. Tabourot/Warlock/
    Gant. Text: French)
14. Les anges dans nos campagnes (French trad., arr. Gant)
15. Hark, the Herald Angels Sing (Mendelssohn, adapted
    Cummings; descant: Willcocks. Text: C.Wesley, adapted
    Whitefield/Madan etc.)
16. The Christ-child's Lullaby (Eriskay trad., arr. Gant)
17. Still, still, still (German, arr. and English text: Gant)
18. Away in a Manger (Melody: Bishop. Text: anon)
19. Away in a Manger (Melody 1: Kirkpatrick. Melody 2:
    Murray. Text: anon, adapted)
20. Personent hodie (from *Piae Cantiones*, 1582)
21. The Twelve Days of Christmas (English trad., arr. Gant)
22. What Child is This? (Music: Gant. Words: Chatterton Dix)
23. We Wish You a Merry Christmas (English trad., arr. Gant)
24. Tempus adest floridum (Spring carol, from *Piae Cantiones*,
    1582, arr. Gant)

VOX TURTURIS

Treble soloists

James Gant

Harry Gant

Sopranos

Ruth Sladden

Sarah Godlee

Alison Coldstream

Sarah Coastworth

Altos

Carol Goodall

James Armitage

Rory McCleery

Timothy Teague

Tenors

Thomas Kelly[†]

Christopher Watson[†]

Tom Phillips[*]

Michael Solomon Williams

Timothy Coleman

Nicholas Keay[*]

Basses

Edward Jones

Dan Sladden

Ed Ballard[†]

Piers Kennedy[†]

Will Dawes[*]

Basil McDonald[*]

Organ

David Quinn

[*]Tracks 1,4,5,10,12,13,14,17,20,21,23 & 24 only
[†]Tracks 2,3,6,7,8,9,11,15,16,18,19 & 22 only

Vox Turturis is a professional chamber choir drawn from leading ensembles based in London and the best young singers, many trained at Oxford and Cambridge Universities. Vox Turturis was founded by Andrew Gant in 2012 with a focus on new choral music. It has given recitals of works by Philip Moore, Paul Spicer, and others. This is Vox Turturis's first recording.

James and Harry Gant are choristers in the Choir of Magdalen College, Oxford.

Andrew Gant is a composer, choirmaster, church musician, university teacher and writer. He has directed many leading choirs including The Guards' Chapel, Worcester College Oxford, and Her Majesty's Chapel Royal. He lectures in Music at St Peter's College, Oxford, and lives in Oxford with his wife and their three children.

·: Index :·

Figures in *italics* indicate illustrations.
Those in **bold** indicate music with text for selected carols.